GETTING OUT

Jonathan Campion

GETTING OUT

The Ukrainian Cricket Team's Last Stand on the Front Lines of War

First published by Pitch Publishing, 2024

Pitch Publishing
9 Donnington Park,
85 Birdham Road,
Chichester,
West Sussex,
PO20 7AJ
www.pitchpublishing.co.uk
info@pitchpublishing.co.uk

A CIP catalogue record is available for this book
from the British Library.

ISBN 978 1 80150 680 9

Typesetting and origination by Pitch Publishing
Printed and bound in India by Replika Press Pvt. Ltd.

CONTENTS

***

For Dad

***

FOREWORD

SPORT IS an integral part of any country and its society; in Ukraine this is no different. Through football, tennis, boxing, athletics and so many other disciplines our sportspeople, whether individuals or in team competitions, have brought inspiration, happiness and pride to millions of Ukrainians for so many years. Even during these times, so many still continue to do so.

In most cases, athletes spend all their childhood training and preparing for potential careers within their sport, making huge sacrifices in other aspects of their lives to prioritise their future ambitions. However, due to circumstances beyond their control, all of that has cruelly become irrelevant at a time like this – a time when our country is being invaded and we, all Ukrainians, have to come together to protect ourselves and each other; our family, friends and the other people closest to us.

Circumstances are different for every sportsperson. Some may have had all their sporting futures still ahead of them, some are in their prime years, and some are in their twilight years. Some perform at a regional level, some at an elite level – but whatever their status, many athletes have had to make the decision to take up arms and put their sense of duty and willingness to protect their country above their own career and personal aspirations.

As an example, Serhiy Stakhovsky, the former world number 31 tennis player, is someone I have known for many years. Shortly after retiring from professional tennis he returned to Ukraine to join the army and protect our country on the front line. As a sign of how quickly and abruptly life can change, mere days passed from the time when Serhiy and I last saw each other to the start of the mass-scale invasion and his return home – away from safety, away from his family – so he could protect his country.

From February 2022, when Russia's mass-scale invasion of Ukraine began, unimaginable horrors have ensued for millions of people. I can only express my gratitude and the highest admiration for all the sportspeople, soldiers and volunteers who are playing some part in the fight to ensure the safety of my family, friends, and the territorial integrity and individual identity of our country.

Unfortunately, a lot of people have had to pay the highest price, and their sacrifices should never be taken for granted. To all of us, they will forever serve as examples of selflessness, courage and true patriotism. Ukraine will never forget its heroes.

I also express my appreciation for Jonathan and all the people around the world who have been putting a spotlight on, as well as helping in any way possible, Ukraine and its people in their fight for survival since the start of Russia's invasion. I only wish that more international sports organisations and governing bodies would do the same to support Ukrainian sport and its athletes, as well as punishing and isolating those of the aggressor, at least to the same extent.

Serhiy Rebrov

Serhiy Rebrov is the manager of Ukraine's national football team. During his playing career he won 75 caps for Ukraine, while playing as a forward for clubs including Shakhtar Donetsk, Dynamo Kyiv, Tottenham Hotspur and Fenerbahçe. He has also managed Dynamo Kyiv, Ferencváros of Hungary, and Dubai's Al-Ain.

Chapter One

LAST MAN IN

'AT NIGHT it was incredibly scary. The whole huge building was like a ghost town. Many nights I was lying there crying. I knew if they hit the building, I'm gone. How will we die? I often thought about that. I always just prayed that it's instant: one big explosion, and then we're gone.'

As Kobus Olivier relives the first days of Russia's invasion of Ukraine in a series of gently spoken voice-notes, he describes the destruction of a country that had unexpectedly become a part of his life. And before the horrors of February 2022 he had also become an unexpected part of Ukrainian life, as the driving force behind Kyiv's junior cricket scene.

The onset of the war came as a sickening twist to a previously charmed life. For three decades Olivier, originally from South Africa, had combined a restless soul with a level three coaching badge to travel the world as a nomadic player and coach. Leaving Cape Town in 1985 to explore the northern hemisphere, Olivier lived in six countries across Europe, Africa and the Middle East, before arriving in Ukraine in 2018, in his late fifties, to be the principal and teach English at the Astor private school in Kyiv.

The move to Eastern Europe was supposed to signal a break from cricket. Ukraine, where the parks are dotted with coffee kiosks, not sets of stumps, seemed like the perfect place for the exhausted Olivier to recover from the burnout of endless nets. But one day in 2018 the cricket bug found him again. For one PE lesson, instead of bringing a football into the sports hall he brought a plastic bat and a tennis ball. His pupils were instantly hooked; before long the children were asking him to play cricket most days. His life began to revolve around the game again. From his seventh-floor apartment in the gritty district of Nyvky, on the western edge of Kyiv, he set about introducing cricket throughout Ukraine, beginning in other private schools.

Ukraine's young cricketers had an influential early supporter. In 2019 Olivier had a chance meeting with Vitali Klitschko, the former world heavyweight boxing champion, and showed him some videos of the children batting and bowling in the school sports hall. Klitschko, now the popular mayor of Kyiv, was impressed with the new game, and arranged for the students to showcase their skills at the city's upcoming summer Festival of Sport.

Throughout the summer festival, Klitchko's department for youth and sport gave the cricketers some space in Syretskiy Park, a big green area in the west of the capital, to play their matches. By 2020, thanks to Olivier's enthusiasm and charisma – and the free English lessons he would give at every practice session – about 2,000 Ukrainians were playing cricket regularly.

By 2021 cricket had made so much progress in Ukraine that Olivier applied for the country to become a member of the International Cricket Council (ICC), the sport's governing body. While only 12 nations play Test matches as ICC Full Members, almost a hundred other countries receive annual funding as Associates, and play international fixtures under the ICC's umbrella. Kobus Olivier's intrepid group of students, bolstered by some older players and expats from cricketing countries, were about to become the world's 108th national cricket team.

Then the Russian missiles came.

The Kremlin's war in Ukraine didn't begin in 2022. At the time when the early cricket games were being played at Astor School and in Syretskiy Park, Russia was already occupying large parts of the country. In 2014 Moscow took control of Crimea, the peninsula on the Black Sea in the south of Ukraine, by holding an unlawful referendum. Soon after a Russian leader was installed in Crimea, Russia's president Vladimir Putin sent troops into the east of Ukraine, to also bring the industrial heartland of Donbas – where more than five million Ukrainians lived in the Luhansk and Donetsk regions – under the control of puppet governments answering to the Kremlin.

Ukraine was in turmoil when, in September 2020, its leader Volodymyr Zelenskiy, the comic actor who was elected president the year before, announced that the country would be entering into a partnership with NATO to ensure its security. The Kremlin reacted by sending tens of thousands of Russian soldiers to military bases close to its border with Ukraine. At the beginning of February 2022 many more troops were sent to these bases, bringing the Russian military presence on Ukraine's border to over 200,000.

Before dawn on the morning of 24 February 2022 the Russian army crossed into Ukraine, and moved in the direction of its largest cities.

Settling into a new home against this backdrop was a far cry from Olivier's previous world. But as our conversations flitted between his past jobs in cricket and the bombings in his neighbourhood, from his love of yoga to his younger days moonlighting as a swimwear model, it becomes clear that he is a man who lives in the moment and doesn't worry too much about tomorrow.

It was inevitable that Olivier would find himself coaching cricket again, even in a place seemingly as removed from the game as Ukraine. The sport was his first love. An opening batter not quite good enough to do it for a living – some matches fielding as 12th man for Western Province, Derbyshire and Kent in the 1980s were the only first-class games he experienced – his energy and patience made him a sought-after coach for youth sides. Lacking the technical skills to coach professional teams, Olivier instead showed a talent for helping children to feel more confident playing the game.

During stints playing league cricket in England and Scotland he became a teacher in the mould of his own mentor, the great coach Bob Woolmer, who was his opening partner for several seasons in club cricket in Cape Town. Later, as the director of cricket at the University of Cape Town, Olivier offered an unknown schoolboy called Graeme Smith a scholarship, and his first captaincy role in senior cricket.

He moved to the Netherlands in 2000 on an invitation from the Dutch Cricket Association to coach the country's youth squads. In two years in Amsterdam he took Dutch junior sides to play in tournaments across northern Europe.

In 2013 Olivier went back to Africa to become the chief executive of Cricket Kenya. The job in Nairobi had him doing everything from preparing the national squad for ICC tournaments to taking cricket to rural schools. But he left after a year to be a coach again, this time at a private school in Dubai.

His salary from the school afforded him a luxury apartment in a glamorous part of Dubai. But by 2018 his feet were itching again. An offer came to go back to East Africa, to Uganda this time, as the CEO of the country's ambitious cricket federation. The post in Kampala would have brought no less prestige, with Uganda's men's team becoming one of the strongest Associate sides in Africa. But after four years in Dubai Olivier couldn't stand the thought of any more heat – or, he had come to realise, any more cricket. His heart was set on a sabbatical in Europe when the offer came to teach at the school in Kyiv.

As much of a culture shock as Ukraine would be for Olivier, a move there wasn't a complete step into the unknown. He had been to Kyiv a few times before, for holidays during his time in Dubai.

As a younger man Kobus had also spent time in Russia. His father's younger brother was South Africa's first ambassador to Russia after the fall of the USSR. Posted to Moscow in the early 1990s, Gerrit Olivier was an advisor to Boris Yeltsin and Nelson Mandela, strengthening ties between a Russia barely functioning under capitalism and a South Africa only starting to dismantle apartheid.

A few months after taking up the job at Astor School in Kyiv came the lesson that changed everything. 'It was getting really difficult', Olivier says in another voice-note, explaining that he was failing as an English teacher. 'The kids weren't paying attention; it was difficult to find new topics that would interest them. We'd done their favourite countries, their pets, their favourite movies ... We were getting bored of each other. Almost in desperation I started talking to them about cricket.'

He took out his phone and showed the class a video on YouTube of one of his favourite players. Seeing a cricketer for the first time, a fielder diving for catches with his right hand outstretched, the Ukrainian children thought he looked like a superhero. They called him 'Batman'. To the students he may have been Batman, but to Olivier, Jonty Rhodes – the world's best fielder in the 1990s – was an old opponent in South Africa. The two had kept in touch, and gone to the gym together whenever Rhodes stayed in Dubai.

The next morning he came to school with a plastic cricket set that he had brought from Dubai. He took his pupils to the indoor sports hall to try cricket for themselves.

The YouTube video left an impression on the new cricketers. 'The guys were unbelievable,' Olivier says. 'In every other country I'd ever coached in, everybody wanted to bat. And these Ukrainian kids didn't want to bat and didn't want to bowl. They just wanted to field like Jonty Rhodes.'

In the following weeks he moved his English lessons from the classroom to the sports hall. He would hit high catches for the students, and they would answer his questions while diving around the gymnasium.

Eventually Olivier managed to persuade the children to bat and bowl as well. 'After a while they started understanding the batting – getting the feel of hitting the ball, the ball flying out of the park. But it was always about fielding for them: they couldn't stop talking about "Batman".'

The success of Vitali Klitchko's Festival of Sport that summer, and the sight of teenagers playing cricket in Syretskiy Park, encouraged other private schools in Kyiv to put cricket on their sports curriculum. By the next year around 2,000 boys and girls were playing cricket in the capital every week.

Klitschko's city department for youth and sport also arranged for Olivier to teach cricket at children's camps, which many young Ukrainians go to during their school holidays. At these camps children stay in hostels and play sports like football, basketball, tennis and volleyball – but from 2019 some of them began to offer cricket lessons as well. During the summer holidays kids batted on the centre circle of football pitches; in winter there were soft-ball games in school sports halls.

But at the beginning of 2022 normal life in Ukraine stopped. Kyiv had been Kobus Olivier's home for four years when the Russian troops began to amass along Ukraine's borders. This show of hostility caused foreign observers to fear that an invasion was imminent.

Olivier's Ukrainian friends, however, were blasé about the threat. In local media the tanks and military units were mostly dismissed as an intimidatory tactic by the Kremlin.

But Olivier, knowing barely a word of the country's languages of Ukrainian and Russian, watched the international news channels, which broadcast images of the troops camping metres away from Ukrainian territory. Tens of thousands of them were in bases only a couple of hours from Kyiv, in the south of Belarus, a close ally of Russia. He was sure that the invasion was going to happen.

In his voice-notes Olivier speaks poignantly about the weeks of anxiety before the terror began. Instead of his usual after-work routine, planning the next day's cricket practice in a cafe behind Independence Square, he began to panic-buy food.

'I knew it was going to happen,' he says. 'I started stocking up two weeks before. Every day I went to the supermarket. I started buying provisions: dry nuts, dry fruit, biscuits; canned food that I could eat cold, like tuna. And I stocked up on litres and litres of water.'

The fields in Belarus where many of the Russian military units were stationed were only 50km (31 miles) north of Kyiv. Looking at maps on his phone, Olivier worked out that their tanks wouldn't be on his TV screen for long: they would soon be in his neighbourhood.

If the artillery heading for the capital were to break through the commuter towns of Irpin and Bucha, their next target would be Nyvky, the district where he lived. Nyvky was only 15km (9 miles) away from Irpin; his building stood next to Peremohy Avenue, the wide boulevard that the tanks would be certain to take as they advanced towards Independence Square in the centre.

He withdrew all of his Ukrainian hryvnia from the bank and changed them into dollars. In his apartment he bundled together his cash, passport and a few possessions, ready to make a quick escape. Then he barricaded himself inside.

'I took my mattress off my bed and put it against the wall, right next to the window,' he tells me. 'The plan was, immediately when the war started and when the first shots came, I was going to put that mattress in front of the window, in case of a missile attack. Flying glass usually causes most of the damage.'

As a batter in South Africa Olivier used to suffer from severe pre-match nerves. He believes that this vulnerability cost him the chance to make a career as a cricketer. But 40 years later in Ukraine, as he realised that he would soon be standing in the middle of a war zone, it was his experience of taking guard against the fast bowlers of Western Cape that helped him to prepare for the inevitable. 'My nerves were in pieces', he says about the wait for the artillery to appear. 'At night I didn't sleep, waiting for explosions. In a way I was relieved that it started, because I knew it was going to happen.

'It was a bit like in my cricket days, when I opened the batting and faced Brian McMillan with a new ball. I used to be scared the day before, and all week I'm building up to Saturday. And then when the Saturday comes I'm actually out there, and he's running in to bowl, and it's almost like "I can deal with it – it's here, it's reality, I have to face it." But the waiting absolutely killed me.'

When the invasion finally did become reality, it didn't take the Russian forces long to reach Irpin. 'On the morning of the 24th when I went for a walk at four in the morning, I heard the first of nine huge explosions right next to my apartment block. I went up to my apartment immediately and put the mattress up. I had a studio apartment. My little lounge and kitchen was all open, so the bathroom was the only room with a door and four walls. I thought I'll lock myself in there.

'It took me ten minutes to get my money, my passport, my documents into the bathroom. And I stayed there for ten days. I literally lived in the bathroom.'

In the coming days marauding Russian soldiers would commit atrocities in Ukrainian towns. Their assault began in the towns outside Kyiv, as well as in the Donbas region in the east of the country. The invaders, many of them teenaged conscripts from deprived regions in Siberia, were told that ethnic Russians living in Ukraine were being repressed by a government controlled by anti-Russian nationalists. In line with the Kremlin's order for the Russian forces to 'liberate Ukraine from Nazis', the young men killed thousands of people during the first wave of the invasion. Most of the victims were unarmed civilians. Hundreds of children lost their lives.

Huddled under blankets in his bathtub, Olivier watched as the orange glow of bombs lit up Kyiv's skyline. 'Irpin was so close to me. I heard huge explosions non-stop during the night, during the day. I heard machine guns – at times there was machine-gun fire right under my balcony. It was a war zone. This wasn't a movie. This was it. This was war.'

Mercifully, the world of professional cricket has not come into contact with war for many decades. Since the end of the Second World War, which took the lives of 139 first-class players, perhaps the only prominent cricketers to be caught in an armed conflict were the Sri Lankan Test team during a tour of Pakistan in 2009. In the middle of a match in Lahore their bus was fired upon by members of the terrorist organisation Lashkar-e-Jhangvi. Eight people were killed in the attack, and many of those involved in the Test match suffered bullet and shrapnel wounds. Sri Lankan players Thilan Samaraweera and Tharanga Paranavitana suffered the worst injuries, while their English coach Paul Farbrace and one of the umpires, Ahsan Raza from Pakistan, were also badly wounded.

In the same year as the Lahore bus attack the Afghanistan cricket team played its first international matches. Many of their first generation of players were born in refugee camps in Pakistan, after their families were displaced by the Soviet-Afghan War in the 1980s.

As Olivier watched television footage of the bombings from his bathroom, the world of sport vanished. Two days before the invasion began, Olivier's class had asked him if they could play another game of cricket together outside on the school's grounds. Now, as the communities on the outskirts of Kyiv came under attack from Russian missiles, the children of Astor School – like millions of Ukrainians – fled with their families over the borders to Poland and Moldova.

Men of fighting age, between 18 and 50, were not permitted to leave Ukraine. Millions of those who couldn't get out of the country tried to travel west, to the cities of Ivano-Frankivsk and Lviv, which the Russian forces had not yet reached. Ukrainians who had no way out of Kyiv resisted the invaders any way they could. From his balcony in Nyvky, Olivier saw old ladies, Ukraine's indestructible *babusi*, striding towards machine-gun-holding soldiers and hurling Molotov cocktails at them.

At night, the complex of eight apartment blocks where Olivier lived was completely empty. Every single resident who had not left the city would run to sleep in one of the city's underground metro stations, which were now being used as bomb shelters.

But Kobus stayed in the building. Protecting himself from the bombings would have meant leaving his four dogs in the apartment alone. Only people were allowed in the bomb shelters, and the crossbreed terriers who had come from Dubai with him, seven-year-old Tiekie and her offspring Ollie, Kaya and Jessie, were his only family.

In the weeks before 24 February he had stocked up on dog food as well. Leaving the four dogs behind was never an option, and the start of the war only strengthened his resolve. 'I told myself: this is it,' he says. 'I'm not leaving my dogs. I'm staying with them, and the reality is we most probably are going to die. I was literally waiting to die. This could be my last hour. It could be our last day together. In a way I had made my peace. I'm going with my dogs. They are my life. We came here together and we'll end this together, whichever way it happens.'

With explosions rocking the neighbourhood, and the apartment block all but empty, Olivier distracted himself during the day by speaking on the phone with the ICC's head of European cricket. Ukraine was four months away from joining the governing body; only the last few boxes needed to be ticked before the next

ICC meeting in July. At night he only had his dogs and some music for company. Olivier played an album by the Croatian cellist Stjepan Hauser to soften the sound of Russian shells outside.

The assault around Irpin intensified in the first week of March. Time was running out: if Kobus didn't leave Kyiv they were certain to die. On 3 March he found a neighbour willing to drive them the 600km (370 miles) west to Ivano-Frankivsk. They spent the next five nights sleeping in the gymnasium of a school that had been turned into a makeshift refugee camp.

On 8 March, as the war spread further, Olivier found a way out of Ukraine. They travelled north-west from Ivano-Frankivsk to cross the border into Poland. A distant acquaintance owned a cottage in the small town of Głowno, in the countryside outside the industrial city of Łódź. He arranged to take refuge there until it was safe to go back to Kyiv.

A new chapter in Poland it would be. But as over two million Ukrainians arrived in Poland in the first weeks of the war, the overwhelmed Polish authorities changed the country's immigration rules so that only Ukrainian citizens could stay there without a residence permit. Olivier had a week to find another country to stay in.

Calming his nerves listening to the Stjepan Hauser album one night, the answer came to him; he would be able to settle in Croatia. Olivier's voice-notes have been coming from Zagreb, the Croatian capital, a full 1,500km (930 miles) to the west of Kyiv.

To make sure that all of his dogs could travel with him, Olivier bought an old Audi Avant, and drove the 1,000km from Głowno to Zagreb. The route took them through Slovakia and Hungary, where they spent two freezing nights sleeping in their lime green car on the Hungary–Croatia border. Eventually, three weeks after leaving Kyiv, they arrived in Zagreb. A little apartment close to the central Zrinjevac Park was mercifully easy to find.

Unpacking his few possessions in Zrinjevac, Kobus Olivier set about applying for a humanitarian visa, and trying to let go of the trauma of the last month. Ten days later, he was playing cricket again.

'The second Saturday I went for a walk in the big park here. I saw these five boys playing football. They were speaking Russian. I went to them and asked if they were from Ukraine by any chance? They said *ja*, they're from Kharkiv, and they were refugees here. I had a little plastic cricket bat that I brought with me from Kyiv, to hit the ball for the dogs. I hit them some catches, let them all have a bat, and they threw the ball to each other. The next time I saw them there were about 12 of them, with their moms, all wanting to play.'

The neighbourhood around Zrinjevac Park, it turned out, was a new home for quite a few other people who had escaped from Ukraine. While Croatia received only a tiny fraction of those who left the country at the start of the war, several hundred Ukrainian mothers and their children arrived in Zagreb during February and March 2022. Some of them came with elderly relatives; almost all of them found themselves staying in the spare rooms of host families. Usually, they had no common language with their hosts. The displaced families were desperate for a chance to socialise, and soothe their aching minds and bodies.

Word soon spread of the bat-and-ball game that some of the Ukrainian children were starting to play in the middle of Zrinjevac Park. Olivier began to arrange cricket practice there three evenings a week, teaching the children and some of their mothers the basics of the game. Knowing that many of the families were struggling to eat enough hot food, after every cricket session at Zrinjevac he would buy three pizzas from a Domino's in one corner of the park.

Before long there were too many children to keep involved with only one bat and one ball. Olivier remembered that while teaching cricket in Ukraine he had made contact with the Lord's Taverners charity in London, which sends cricket equipment to children who wouldn't otherwise be able to play. The Taverners had shipped eight boxes of cricket kit to Kyiv, but because of a problem with the customs paperwork the boxes had got stuck in a warehouse somewhere in Lithuania. Olivier had the bats, balls and other equipment sent to Zagreb instead.

By May 2022 there were over 13,000 Ukrainian refugees in Croatia. Throughout the summer over 150 Ukrainian children were playing soft-ball cricket games in Zrinjevac Park every other afternoon, running around in Sussex CCC beanie hats and wearing Slazenger wicketkeeping gloves.

'Of course it wasn't just cricket,' says Olivier in another voice-note. 'It was trauma treatment for the kids. Most of them were from Mariupol, Kharkiv, Severodonetsk, those areas [that came under the most intense bombing]. Later on we had quite a few from Kyiv. They had seen the worst of the war. Their fathers were all stuck in Ukraine. They couldn't leave the country, because they were fighting age. These kids and their moms were terribly traumatised. So it became like a support group for the mothers.'

Not all of the mothers stayed on the boundary to watch their children. Olivier adds: 'While the kids were playing cricket a lot of the moms helped. One of our success stories was that one of the mothers, Anna, went online and completed the whole ICC Foundation coaching course. She did everything herself, without telling me or anyone else. When she got her certificate, she became the first ICC-certified coach from Ukraine.'

As the eighth chapter of a nomadic life, perhaps it was inevitable that Olivier would find himself teaching cricket in Croatia, just as it had been four years earlier in Ukraine. 'I can't escape cricket,' he said one evening, as his newest pupils finished their pizza in the park. 'And cricket can't escape me'.

Chapter Two

GOOD REVOLUTIONS

THE MASSIVE anti-government protests in the winter of 2013, when up to 800,000 people gathered in Kyiv's Independence Square (Maidan Nezalezhnosti), gave Ukraine a new energy. By February 2014 the country's corrupt president Viktor Yanukovych had been thrown out of power, in what came to be known as the Maidan Revolution.

Yanukovych was a former governor of the eastern city of Donetsk, who had spent time in prison twice in his youth for violent assaults. As president he and his prime minister, Yulia Tymoshenko, mired Ukrainian business and politics even deeper in bribery and fraud. He also tried to realign the country with Russia, in doing so burning several of Ukraine's fragile bridges with the European Union. The uprising that brought Petro Poroshenko to power in 2014, which Ukrainians call the Revolution of Dignity, gave Ukraine its direction back. It also gave Kyiv another cricket pitch.

Yanukovych lived in a plush neighbourhood called Mezhyhirya on the northern edge of Kyiv. His residence overlooked Astor School, where Kobus Olivier would one day come to teach. In the weeks after Yanukovych fled the country, some members of the public realised that there was no one guarding his mansion. When they walked into the former president's home they found some absurd things there: pet ostriches strolling around an outdoor pen; bottles of luxury Armenian brandy with his own face on the label; and papers detailing colossal corruption floating on the top of a lake.

He also left behind his private nine-hole golf course. Four years later – with the criminal Yanukovych still in hiding in Russia and charged with treason against Ukraine – Olivier planted a set of cricket stumps on one of his greens, to turn part of the abandoned course into a cricket square.

Of all the schools and summer camps to have taken up cricket, Mezhyhirya had the most picturesque outfield. As the children hit their shots out on to the old fairways, the ball often flew near herds of deer and hares. Games were sometimes stopped in the middle of an over by flocks of ducks waddling past the stumps.

Youth cricket in Ukraine was different to the other countries where Olivier had coached. To his surprise, he found that in every school the girls were much stronger players than the boys. 'Most of the girls in Ukraine do some kind of dancing or gymnastics,' he explains. 'Rhythmic gymnastics, ballet ... so even at a young age their coordination is unbelievable. These young girls had unbelievable rhythm, and their bodies were incredibly strong and supple from their gymnastics. Although the boys played football, the girls were more suited to cricket. They were streets ahead.'

Eight of Kyiv's private schools had girls' cricket teams, and these teams often played soft-ball matches against each other. In 2021 there were more active female players in Ukraine than there are in many established cricketing nations. Outside of the ICC's Test match-playing countries, the girls' cricket leagues were almost unique, in that all of the players were learning the game in their own country.

'The girls had potential,' Olivier says. 'With proper coaching, by the time they were 17 they would really have been able to play in ICC age-group tournaments. In five years' time I was 100% convinced they would beat a South African under-17 girls team. Before the war I told the ICC that we could be a force in women's cricket in five to six years.'

Because the Astor School was one of the country's most prestigious academies, many of Kobus Olivier's young cricketers were the children of Ukraine's elite. The school's best batter also had first-class sporting genes: Daryna Pyatova is the eldest daughter of Andriy Pyatov, the Shakhtar Donetsk goalkeeper who won over 100 caps for Ukraine. 'From all the youngsters I coached there,' Olivier remembers, 'she was by far the best. She hit the ball miles; she just had unbelievable natural hand-eye coordination. And her catching skills were phenomenal; she obviously played quite a bit of football with her dad.

'She was by far the best cricketer in the school. I told her that if she focuses on cricket and gets some proper coaching she'll be a top, top player one day. She could have been right up there with the best in the world, I'm convinced of that.'

Olivier's class played cricket on the golf course all year round. In the winter, when the temperature fell to ten degrees below freezing and the snow on the fairways was shin-deep, the students still wanted to practise before classes, if only by bowling snowballs to each other. As Olivier planned his cricket lessons in the cafe behind Maidan Nezalezhnosti, he was writing his name into the history of cricket, as the man who introduced the sport to Ukraine.

Or so he thought. What he didn't know during those cold mornings in Mezhyhirya was that cricket had already been played in the country for 25 years. One day in 2019 he received a call out of the blue from the father of Ukrainian cricket: a businessman in the eastern city of Kharkiv named Hardeep Singh.

A pace bowler during his childhood in India, Singh had been organising cricket in Kharkiv since he was 20. After moving to Ukraine in the early 1990s to study at university, he had brought together some other Indian students for quick games of cricket in the parks outside the city. These evening slogs were played with a tennis ball wrapped in electrical tape, like in so many scratch games in Asia, and gave his compatriots a chance to socialise, and stave off their homesickness. Eventually Singh attracted enough players to arrange tape-ball leagues in the city.

When he graduated in 1995 Singh stayed in Kharkiv. He set up a company that arranged for students from India and other countries to study at Ukrainian universities, as he himself once had. In 2000 he created the Ukrayinska Federatsiya Kriketu, the Ukraine Cricket Federation (UCF), with its headquarters at his office on Serpova Street. By the time word reached him of the South African teaching Ukrainians to play cricket in Kyiv, he had coached several intakes of good

Asian cricketers, from those young people who had signed up to his study programmes.

Now in his mid-forties but still a big presence in the competitive Kharkiv leagues as a batter and gun fielder, Singh had also set his sights on his adopted home becoming a member of the ICC. Joining the ICC would bring cricket in Ukraine some vital funding and resources; but more importantly, it would allow a team to represent the country in official international matches. The men's and women's squads would be able to enter the qualifying stages for the Twenty20 (T20) World Cups, where their runs and wickets, catches and stumpings would be recorded on ESPNcricinfo forever. The Ukraine men's national team would enter the T20 world rankings, just below the Seychelles, Panama and Bhutan.

But Singh knew he wasn't going to get anywhere with a team full of Indian students; he needed proof that there were some local cricketers in Ukraine. Rather than treating Olivier as a rival, he was calling to suggest that they join forces, to make the dream of some truly national cricket teams happen together.

The pair disliked each other almost from the first meeting, but the uneasy partnership gave both of them what they wanted. As the UCF's president, Singh had the services of the best qualified cricket coach in

Eastern Europe, who had passionately grown grassroots cricket in the Netherlands and Kenya. Olivier received an extra €1,000 a month to top up his teacher's salary, and the lofty title of chief executive of the UCF.

As it was for Olivier, cricket was Singh's first love. Born in the town of Jalandhar, he was called up to Punjab's youth teams in the 1980s as a quick bowler, before a back injury in his late teens derailed his cricket career. He took to business instead, and his ventures in Ukraine made him a millionaire. As well as his company that offered university courses, BobTrade Education Group, he owned the India Palace restaurant on Matyushenka Street in the centre of Kharkiv, and several properties in the city. In Kharkiv the foreign students lived in dormitory buildings that he owned.

Outside of the country it is often assumed that the population of Ukraine is entirely white and Slavic, but for decades there have been large diasporas from Asia and Africa in all of its cities. Many of the international guests are students pursuing degrees in medicine and engineering; the quality of teaching in Ukraine is high, while fees to study at the best universities are much cheaper than in Western Europe. Degrees from Kyiv, Kharkiv and elsewhere give Asian and African students a chance to build careers in their own countries as European-qualified doctors and engineers.

Nevertheless, moving to Ukraine has always been an overwhelming prospect for young people from outside Europe. Winters are painful, reaching 20 and more degrees below freezing, and cities have often been dangerous places for foreigners. Against this background, Hardeep Singh's businesses became a calling card for Kharkiv.

As the boys and girls signing up for BobTrade study programmes thought about moving halfway across the world, they were comforted to know that there would be some biryani and cricket waiting for them when they got there.

Ukraine and India have at least a few things in common. For one, the Ukrainian language uses the Urdu word *maidan* for a meeting place or square. But while in India the word 'maidan' brings to mind an urban park where cricket matches are played, in Ukraine it is a paved space in the centre of a city, as in Kyiv's Maidan Nezalezhnosti, the Independence Square where the 2014 revolution came to a boil.

In the middle of the 1990s cricket in Ukraine slowly spread from Kharkiv to other cities. By the time the schoolchildren played their matches at Vitali Klitchko's summer festival in 2019, Kyiv already had a busy cricket community. As Hardeep Singh had become the father of cricket in Kharkiv in 1993, so the pharmaceutical executive Thamarai Pandian took the same steps in the capital four years later.

Ukraine was Pandian's home for 26 years, after his company sent him there in 1997. But when we speak in March 2023 the war has forced him back to India. He is in Chennai, the city where, as a young man, he was a good all-rounder in schools cricket, a competitive footballer and middle-distance runner, and a field hockey player talented enough to represent India at junior level.

Cricket in mid-1990s Kyiv, Pandian explains, was a game that only a few foreigners knew about. 'By and large the first players came from the student community in Kyiv,' he tells me on a video call. 'They were all Indians. We started playing with a taped tennis ball, and slowly the interest developed. Kyiv Polytechnic Institute let us use their stadium. We imported a matting wicket and all the equipment from India and played our matches there.'

The stadium at the institute was a sports pitch used by students and staff at the nearby college of civil aviation. Kyiv's first games of cricket were played on a wide field surrounded by shallow banks of concrete seats.

With the end of Ukraine's first decade of independence bringing a measure of stability under president Leonid Kuchma, and a handful of international companies setting up in the country, the first cricket tournaments held at the institute ground were rather grand events. 'In 1999 and 2000 the Indian businesses in Kyiv supported us with huge funds,' says Pandian of the dawn of Ukrainian T20. 'We had some really competitive cricket, with 10 to 12 teams. And the prize money was amazing: something like two or three thousand US dollars for the winners. The tournament's best player would get $500.

'We had students and expats coming from all over Ukraine to play and we had so many people supporting the sport: the British and Indian ambassadors were among our patrons. The South African ambassador at that time was also a great supporter.'

From 2000 onwards, Pandian's contacts in the corporate world – he was by now the head of a big pharma company's operations in Eastern Europe – allowed him to take the cricket games much more seriously. Together with the British ambassador to Ukraine at the time, Roland Smith, he formed the Kyiv Cricket Club. The team soon had a few rivals, including a side from the British-Ukrainian Chamber of Commerce.

The stadium at the polytechnic institute staged two tournaments each year – one at the start of summer and one at the end. Their main sponsor in the early days was one of Ukraine's most popular consumer brands, the powdered drink MacCoffee.

Tournament fixtures were spread over consecutive weekends, and Pandian smiles as he describes the jolliness of it all. 'It was usually more like a carnival. It would be like a family get-together; August and September is barbecue time in Kyiv.' One of the city's Indian restaurants, New Bombay Palace, supplied the food for the barbecues.

Whenever the stadium at the polytechnic was unavailable, Pandian's cricketers looked for other unused sports pitches around the city. Often they rolled out their portable matting wicket in the middle of the Voskhod stadium, a dilapidated 10,000-capacity football and athletics ground in Kyiv's eastern district of Darnytsia. It was here that Pandian held the early editions of the Kyiv Cricket League, a T20 competition where his Kyiv CC played against a 'Friends XI', 'Boss XI', 'Khan XI' and a 'Seniors XI'.

Eventually cricketers began to travel from other parts of Ukraine to take part in the tournaments. The student sides that Hardeep Singh sent to play for Kharkiv were almost permanent fixtures in the semi-finals. Although no one ever knew why, a lot of strong Asian cricketers also ended up studying in Luhansk.

The matches in the early 2000s were still only fought between expats – mainly Indians, with the occasional Australian and Brit drifting in – but on the other side of the boundary Ukrainian guests were starting to pick up bats and balls too. 'We invited Ukrainian children to come and play,' remembers Pandian. 'School classes would come with their physical education teachers. We printed a lot of leaflets in Ukrainian and Russian, with the basic rules: what are runs, what are wickets … we used to have a lot of spectators; it was a new sport, something different.'

Eventually the Ukrainians' catching and hitting on the sidelines became too good to ignore. In 2003 Singh and Pandian made a rule that there should be a Ukrainian player in every team. The next year this was increased to two; it was also agreed that the local players must either bowl two overs in a game, or bat in the top four. The Ukrainians never featured at the top of the runs or wickets charts, but their catching and fielding never let anyone down.

A couple of years later, a man named Yuri Zahurskiy became the first Ukrainian cricketer to really go toe-to-toe with the Indians. Coming from a rural community about an hour south of Kyiv, where he worked for a business that produces biofuels, Zahurskiy taught himself to bat when some Australian friends introduced him to the game. Years later, in the first days of the invasion when the Russian artillery reached the outskirts of Kyiv, the legend of Yuri Zahurskiy would extend far beyond the cricket pitch.

Most of Kyiv's cricketers were born in other countries, but every one of them resolutely called Ukraine home. Many were Ukrainian passport-holders and dual citizens. Most worked at Ukrainian companies and spoke fluently with colleagues, while several, like Hardeep Singh, had Ukrainian spouses, and children born in the country. As the seasons passed the expat vibe disappeared: by 2005 tournaments featured teams with names like Taras Shevchenko CC (named after Ukraine's national poet), and Bohomolets (The Pilgrims).

Nor was it only men who played cricket. The trailblazer for women's cricket in Kyiv was a Ukrainian lady called Inna Illingworth, who fell in love with cricket in the early 2010s while going to watch her English husband play. The tournaments that the Ukraine Cricket Federation organised often included women's competitions, and female players always shared its grounds and equipment. It was Inna who organised training and matches for women.

Inna's husband John, a Yorkshireman, spent most of the decade working in Kyiv as a telecommunications executive, and opened the bowling for the British-Ukrainian Chamber of Commerce. John Illingworth, the side's captain, came with some cricketing pedigree: his uncle Raymond Illingworth played 61 Tests for England, leading them to an Ashes series win away in Australia in 1971, and took over 2,000 first-class wickets.

Ray Illingworth never came to Kyiv to see his nephew play, but when Pandian held his summer tournaments there was often an international player or two watching on the sidelines. In 2007 a Sri Lankan businessman in Ukraine brought his friend Marvan Atapattu to Kyiv to spend three days with the players, a few months before the opener flew to Australia to play the last of his 90 Tests. In other years Kyiv's cricketers shared stories at the Voskhod stadium with Jeevan Mendis, an all-rounder who played 80 times for Sri Lanka, and Farokh Engineer, who was India's charismatic wicketkeeper in the 1960s and 70s.

A couple of years after Atapattu's visit, Ukrainian cricket took another step forward when another big sponsor came on board. In 2010 the *Kyiv Post*, the country's biggest English-language newspaper, gave the UCF a large sum of money to host its summer cricket festivals. The newspaper moved the matches from the shabby Voskhod stadium to the professional arena of the capital's second football team, Obolon Kyiv.

That year the *Kyiv Post* organised an Ambassadors' Cup, where the guests of honour were the Pakistani ambassador to Ukraine, Ghazanfar Ali Khan, and his British counterpart Leigh Turner CMG. Another special guest was the former Olympic champion pole vaulter Serhiy Bubka, who was the head of Ukraine's National Olympic Committee. For the occasion the cricketers played on the immaculate grass of the Obolon Arena, and swapped their coloured clothes for whites, and their between-innings Indian takeaway for Pimm's and cucumber sandwiches.

It shouldn't have been a surprise that the owner of the *Kyiv Post* turned out to be useful with the bat himself. Although he was educated in Donetsk, and came to prominence as the owner of Donetsk Steel Mill, Mohammad Zahoor had grown up in Karachi, Pakistan. Before he became one of Ukraine's wealthiest people, making around $1 billion from the sale of the steel mill, Zahoor had been a keen cricketer, playing as an off-spinner in England as well as in Pakistan.

A few hours after Zahoor scored some runs for Kyiv CC, his team's captain Thamarai Pandian was receiving the winners' trophy from the Ukrainian pop singer Kamaliya. Kamaliya, Zahoor's wife, is also an actress, and was crowned the 2008 Mrs World. The couple raises a great deal of money for orphanages and heart hospitals in Ukraine through the Kamaliya and Mohammad Zahoor Charitable Foundation. Since 2022 Mr Zahoor, who has lived in Russia, and Kamaliya, who was born there, have also bought F-16 fighter jets for the Ukrainian Armed Forces.

Meanwhile, the handful of Ukrainian cricketers were going from strength to strength, at least when it came to their batting. In 15 years, cricket in Ukraine had been transformed from tape-ball slogs between Indian students to a sport for all nationalities and generations. When the newspaper owner brought his three nephews to play in tournaments, and the biofuel developer brought his two sons, there ensued a multilingual battle between the Zahoors and the Zahurskiys.

It was around this time that Ukraine's cricketers hosted their first foreign team. In June 2012 some social cricketers from Hertfordshire in England travelled to Kyiv to watch some games at the European football championships, which Ukraine hosted jointly with Poland. The friends found out that some cricket was played in Kyiv, and got in touch with Thamarai Pandian to set up a couple of T20 fixtures during their trip. A Ukrainian invitation team was quickly put together.

The Englishmen had met each other when their children went to Manland Primary School in Harpenden. They had been playing and touring together in Britain for years – but if they were hoping for some easy runs and wickets at the Voskhod stadium they were soon put in their place. In the first match the Ukraine XI scored 227, before bowling out Manland Dads CC for 88.

The tourists crossed the Dnipro river the next day to go to a more impressive stadium, the Olimpiyskiy, for a quarter-final of Euro 2012. That night ended with another English loss, as Italy knocked out Roy Hodgson's team on penalties. When the friends went back to the cricket pitch in Darnytsia two days later to play their second match, Pandian, perhaps taking pity on them, put out a seniors XI. It made for a closer game than the first T20, albeit the home team won it as well.

The consolation prize for the Manland Dads – besides another of their hosts' biryani teas – was a 10-minute segment about their cricket tour to Ukraine on BBC Radio's *Test Match Special*. During the interval of England's T20 match against West Indies at Trent Bridge that week, Simon Mann cut away to a BBC journalist who was in Kyiv to cover the football, and had popped into the Voskhod to watch the cricket.

Once the journalist had got over the stadium's crumbling concrete stands and bumpy turf – 'Well, Lord's it certainly is not ... I don't know when the floodlights were last used ...' – he ended up interviewing some of the players. One of the English team, it turned out, had studied in Ukraine in the 1990s: he mentioned that there was a cricket team in Donetsk, as well as in the town of Simferopol in Crimea.

Listening to the *TMS* segment in 2023, 11 years after it was recorded, it is striking to hear how optimistic people felt about Ukraine just over a decade ago. Two years after Euro 2012, and the English friends' carefree sporting trip to the country, both Donetsk and Crimea would fall under Russian occupation.

A photograph on the Manland Dads CC website shows the team on Kyiv's central boulevard, Khreshchatyk, in full cricket whites, standing in front of a statue of Lenin. As they pose with the team's flag, three pike fish on a red and green background, four members of Ukraine's armed riot police in the background give them confused but unbothered glances.

Among the Kyiv expats who used to pop into the Voskhod stadium to watch the cricket matches, a regular spectator was a thirty-something former cobbler from Leeds called Sean Carr. Carr was better known in Yorkshire as the lead singer of the thrash metal band the

Death Valley Screamers, with a private life as gruesome as his music.

Rumours about his chequered past followed him to Kyiv, but after moving to Ukraine his life took an unexpected turn. In 2005 he married Yevhenia Tymoshenko, the daughter of the new prime minister Yulia Tymoshenko. They formed Ukraine's oddest celebrity couple: when they weren't running their Italian restaurant in the centre of the city, or watching the cricket, the pair travelled around the country on Carr's Harley-Davidson motorcycle.

The couple divorced in 2011; Carr left Ukraine soon after, and died in Prague in 2018. Most of the cricketers who appeared in the country's first few tournaments also left Ukraine long before the 2022 invasion. But Thamarai Pandian still calls Kyiv home. He tells me from Chennai that he is planning to return to Kyiv in the summer of 2023, whether Russian missiles are still hitting the capital or not.

Against the odds, the city developed a lot in the decade before the invasion began. The Maidan Revolution was a catalyst for Kyiv to modernise and connect with the rest of Europe. The people of Kyiv have changed too since the start of the millennium, when Pandian had to hand out paper flyers to promote his foreign sport. Now the internet, with trending topics on social media, and online betting gives people all over the world a gateway to cricket. 'Just before the war a lot of Ukrainians had heard about the IPL [Indian Premier League],' Pandian tells me. 'Thanks to that quite a few of them began playing.'

Cricket appeared very briefly in the media in 2016, when the country's top sportsperson tried her hand at it. When the tennis player Elina Svitolina came to Australia at the end of the year for two hard court tournaments, the Brisbane Heat, who were midway through their season in Australia's Big Bash T20 competition, invited her to join their squad for a practice session.

A few Ukrainian sports websites shared a video that the Women's Tennis Association (WTA) posted online, of Svitolina playing in the nets at the Gabba stadium. Batting left-handed in a pair of the team's turquoise pads, the girl from Odesa hit some straight drives off the back foot. She middled some throw-downs from the squad's young reserve all-rounder, Marnus Labuschagne.

The media day link-up seemed to bring everyone luck. Brendon McCullum's Brisbane Heat, fresh from hooking the tennis balls that the then world number 16 had served at them with her racquet, beat the Hobart Hurricanes the next day. Svitolina, no longer swinging a Kookaburra, made the semi-finals of that week's

Brisbane International. After making the third round of the Australian Open a few weeks later she reached a career-high number three in the world.

It wasn't Elina Svitolina's first taste of cricket. While dating the England pace bowler Reece Topley she had watched some of his matches for Hampshire. In 2017 she told the *Independent* newspaper about her connections to the game: 'There were a couple of players that tried to explain it to me. I didn't understand it. Now it's much better. Reece's dad explained it a little bit more. At their house they have a net, so I had a little hit in there, using my backhand. I'm not that good; I'm trying to learn more.'

In later years Ukrainian cricketers took Thamarai Pandian's place in playing XIs. After retiring from playing he became the go-to umpire for the country's biggest matches. The social side to the game in Kyiv may have been convivial, but from time to time the words on the pitch would turn ugly. More often than not the confrontations were caused by biased umpiring.

Pandian also gave more time to his role as the UCF's vice-president, becoming more involved in Ukraine's application to join the ICC. He tells me near the end of our call: 'We had a dream that one day Ukraine would be on the ICC map. I'm very proud that I have been part of the journey from the start.'

As more Ukrainian adults came to turn out for the senior sides in Kyiv, Kobus Olivier was busy coaching the players of the future. With no shop in the country selling cricket equipment, the children at Kyiv's schools, like the pupils playing on the golf course in Mezhyhirya, got their bats and balls from the most intriguing of sources. In summer 2022 my phone pinged with a message from an unknown number. In the avatar was a tall, lithe man in a crisp white dress shirt and waistcoat, smiling at a formal function with Sachin Tendulkar.

It isn't easy to say which of the two men has more friends in the world of cricket. Shyam Bhatia is the founder of Alam Steel, one of the largest metals companies in the Middle East. Raised in India, where he played cricket for Rajasthan and Saurashtra, Bhatia moved to Dubai in the 1960s. Now in his eighties, he is still one of the most successful businessmen in the United Arab Emirates.

The former batter has also spent decades helping cricket to take root in new places. The cricket sets that he shipped to schools in Ukraine came through his charity foundation Cricket for Care, which had previously kitted out the fledgling cricket associations of Japan, Thailand and Indonesia.

Bhatia also sends equipment to Test-playing countries in Africa and Asia, for children in government schools and rural clubs that can't afford to buy their own kit. His idea is to bring cricket to those who wouldn't otherwise be able to play, with the belief that the sport teaches children human qualities, like discipline, teamwork and leadership, that are needed to become successful in any walk of life.

Bhatia is visiting London for a few days, and invites me to meet him at his hotel in Mayfair. I ask him how the young cricketers he saw when he visited Kyiv compared with the children he had seen play in ICC-supported countries like Pakistan, South Africa and Zimbabwe. Bhatia tells me: 'They had the same talent … but then you have to coach them.' And in Ukraine that was where Kobus Olivier, who Bhatia had crossed paths with in Dubai and Kenya, came in.

Bhatia knows talent when he sees it. On rare occasions he has given grants to junior cricketers in India that catch his eye. In 2009 he gave one such award to a 12-year-old Sarfaraz Khan, who has since become a prolific first-class batter for Mumbai.

Bhatia's obsession with cricket doesn't stop at the grassroots game: there can't be many international cricketers who don't know who he is. He is known in professional circles for the private cricket museum he built at his residence in Dubai. The museum is a treasure trove of rare books, as well as a display of bats and other personal items signed by Sachin Tendulkar,

Imran Khan, Anil Kumble, Javed Miandad, Joe Root and others. From his friend Syed Kirmani came one of his favourite items – the gloves that the wicketkeeper wore when India won the 1983 World Cup.

Since its opening in 2010, most teams playing in series in the UAE have been invited for a walk with Bhatia around his museum. The names in his guest book would make up a formidable World XI, led by his close friend Sunil Gavaskar ('Fantabulous'), and with greetings from Allan Donald ('If I had a place like this I would sleep in it'), Kapil Dev ('Hope to come back again'), Steve Waugh ('A fantastic tribute to cricket') and Kumar Sangakkara ('The passion and love that is visible is touching').

Bhatia was invited to be the patron of Ukrainian cricket. He may count some of the all-time greats as friends, but as I was to find out later, he also looked after the unknown cricketers of Ukraine, both before and during the Russian invasion.

Chapter Three

OVER THE LINE

WHEN THE congregation of the Calvary Chapel church in the small town of Kaharlyk arrived for an early morning service one Sunday in 2019, they were greeted with a shock. As the families approached the building, a strong smell of curry was drifting through the doors.

When they entered the hall they found about 50 dark-skinned men, some changing into sports kit, some still sleeping on the pews. It was no use complaining to the church leader about the intruders and their food: it was Pastor Wayne Zschech who had organised the church's cricket festival.

Zschech grew up on the east coast of Australia, by the tropical sea of Queensland's Hervey Bay, but has Ukrainian roots, his ancestors having moved to Australia from Ukraine. He came to their country for the first time as a 17-year-old in 1993, to spend a year as a missionary in the newly independent Ukraine. Thirty years later he is still in Kaharlyk, a town of about 10,000 people 80km (50 miles) south of Kyiv.

Since the war in the east of Ukraine began in 2014, Zschech has also worked to secure humanitarian aid for the people whose lives are being endangered. He is a field leader for the Christian organisation Operation Mobilisation, for whom he went back to Australia with his wife Olha and their four children in 2022 to raise donations for communities that are being destroyed and isolated by the Russian attacks.

Until the invasion the 47-year-old had been a leader of a different kind. Zschech was the founder and captain of the first native Ukrainian cricket team, and the groundsman at Ukraine's first dedicated cricket ground.

Growing up in Hervey Bay, Zschech beams on a video call from Kaharlyk, he was a stylish left-handed batter. He had a classical technique, but by his own admission the only awards he ever won were prizes for keenness.

Throwing himself into his new life in the church in rural Ukraine, Zschech was resigned to the idea that he would never play cricket again. 'Cricket was dead for me; it didn't exist,' he says. 'I didn't have cable television or the internet. It just had to disappear from my life.'

That was until the day in 2008 when an acquaintance from Tasmania told him about Thamarai Pandian's matches in Kyiv. The next weekend he drove to the capital, dressed in the closest clothes he could find to cricket whites, and hoped that his forward defence was still in order.

In his thirties at the time, Zschech hadn't watched any cricket for 15 years. In his mind the game was still as he knew it in late-1980s Queensland. What he found at the Voskhod stadium was a world away from that. 'I turned up to Kyiv and it was this terrible soccer field,' he tells me. 'Spring was trying to come through but it was still cold. The field was full of divots from soccer, and it was sandy and muddy. Suddenly I got tossed the white ball: *white* ball, coloured clothes; "twenty-twenty", whatever that was … As Christians we say that people can be born again: well, for me this was like a new birth experience!'

After an afternoon watching the Asian players fizzing a tape-ball around a bumpy field, he knew that if he wanted to keep up with them, he needed to reinvent himself. To make a go of playing cricket in Ukraine he would have to be less Allan Border, and more Adam Gilchrist.

After a few more matches, Zschech did what anyone would have done after their first season of cricket in 15 years. He had a bowling machine shipped to Kaharlyk, borrowed a bat from his Tasmanian acquaintance, converted a long barn where he had been growing mushrooms into an indoor net, and spent all his free hours whacking straight sixes over the machine.

He found that batting was great for easing the stress that came with being a community leader in Ukraine. The country at the start of the millennium was still being dragged down by corruption and maddening bureaucracy. Any projects in Kaharlyk that involved dealing with government bodies made even the town's Australian pastor lose his temper.

Zschech remembers: 'There's something really satisfying about smashing a cricket ball. Over one winter I went from being this guy who was struggling to play Twenty20 in Kyiv, to getting a 3lb 5oz bat from this Tasmanian guy and just bunting the ball over the bowler.'

As his blood pressure came down, his batting average shot up. 'So the next season starts up in Kyiv,' he says, 'and suddenly I'm one of the super-hot players, because I've been practising all winter.' Tall and athletically built, Zschech looks every bit a top-order batter.

His work has kept him fit, too. As well as being the pastor at Calvary Chapel he runs the sustainability initiative 'Chysta Dusha, Chyste Misto' (Clean Soul, Clean City), which turns various kinds of waste into biofuels and other useful resources. This energy is then used to power buildings in Kaharlyk and other towns.

The technologies that Zschech and his team have developed, called pyrolysis, are able to convert discarded plastics into electricity and engine fuels, turn municipal waste into electricity and heating fuel, and change biomass into electricity, fertilisers and heating for greenhouses.

Ukraine has badly needed ecological startups like 'Clean Soul' for decades, but Zschech's breakthroughs are now crucial to a country at war, where people are often hit with electricity blackouts, and are forced to rely on food that they grow themselves.

Over the winter of 2009, Zschech realised that he didn't need to keep the net for himself. Nor did he need to travel all the way to Kyiv whenever he wanted to play a match. The thought came to him that cricket would be good for the community in Kaharlyk – for the Ukrainians who came to his church, as well as the foreigners in the region who may not have many opportunities to socialise. Cricket seemed a perfect way to put his Christian values into practice.

His first convert to the sport was Yuri Zahurskiy. As well as being members of the same church, Zschech and Zahurskiy are friends, and business partners at the 'Clean Soul' initiative. Zahurskiy joined the project soon after it began, and has been involved with it ever since.

He is the man who would come to hold his own against Ukraine's best foreign-born cricketers. Born in a village in the Chernihiv region in the north-east of the country, he doesn't look like a natural sportsman – Zschech describes him as 'a fridge of a bloke' – but during a hit-around at a barbecue in Kaharlyk in 2010 Zahurskiy revealed some serious reflexes.

One of the Australian guests at the barbecue returned home soon after, and shipped Yuri a cricket bat: a bulky County 555. Zschech and Zahurskiy went straight to the mushroom barn to try it out; as his friend the pastor batted left-handed, that's how Yuri held the bat as well.

Zahurskiy was about 40 at the time. He and Wayne Zschech invited their congregation and some of their neighbours to join their net sessions in the barn, and it wasn't long before there were almost enough players for a team. One of the keenest juniors was Yuri's eldest son Petro (Petya to his friends); there were also the Slinko brothers, Serhiy (Seryozha) and Volodymyr (Vova).

That summer Zschech spoke with the mayor of Kaharlyk, and asked him if some space in the town could be allocated for a cricket field. The request was filed at the mayor's office; of course, he didn't receive a response.

But the cricketers kept playing. In the warm months Zschech took the bowling machine outside and played with his congregation in a field behind the church. He installed an outdoor net between two houses for them to practice in, complete with an astroturf wicket with white lines to mark the creases. The church became their pavilion, and as news about the new cricket club spread outside of the town, players would come for the weekend and stay there.

'The church is a two-storey building,' Zschech explains. 'We put in rooms for refugees during the first war [in 2014]. Suddenly people could come [from other parts of the country] and have practice with us.' Often these guests were Indian Christians living in nearby cities.

Player numbers continued to grow. 'While we were practising,' Zschech tells me, 'the town was beginning to take notice a little bit.' Young Ukrainians would walk into the field to join them, but when they arrived in the net they didn't expect that someone would give them a ball to throw; they assumed that the men shouting in a cage, wearing armour and helmets, were some kind of gladiators. Some older villagers didn't understand that the nets had anything to do with sport: Zschech laughs as he remembers that 'they thought that the cage we'd put up was for an emu farm!'

Kaharlyk is as nondescript a place as they come, surrounded by flat arable fields and derelict Soviet farms. When Wayne Zschech arrived as a missionary in 1993 he found a community in near poverty, struggling with unemployment and alcoholism. Ukraine's development in the last ten years breathed life into the town, allowing initiatives such as Operation Mobilisation and 'Clean Soul, Clean City' to grow. Nevertheless, even before the invasion of 2022, life in Kaharlyk was far from easy.

The few people who have heard of the place know it from the dystopian novel *Kaharlyk* by the satirical author Oleh Shynkarenko. Published in 2014, at the time of Russia's seizure of Crimea and Donbas, Kaharlyk is the setting for a story that imagines life in Ukraine a hundred years in the future, where a century of Russian occupation has taken the country back to the Middle Ages.

In *Kaharlyk* the protagonist, Ivan, has his memory erased by the enemy, who used his brain to control its space satellites. He goes to the town to search for his wife, Olena. On some winter days, one of the more dystopian visions in real-life Kaharlyk was the sight of the town's church leader taking his congregation out into a snow-covered field and clearing a wicket for games of ice cricket.

Batting on ice must have been a very different proposition to taking guard on a grass pitch. A photograph from one of the games shows a batter in a woolly hat, batting with only two fielders on the leg side, and five mid-offs, all wearing fur-lined coats.

In 2012 the players received a little miracle. The town's mayor got back in touch with Zschech to say that he had found a field for Kaharlyk Cricket Club to play matches on. A new neighbourhood was being built a couple of kilometres from the church, which would eventually include a school. Construction on the school building hadn't begun, and until it opened, the oval that would be its sports field wasn't being used for anything. If Zschech wanted, he could lease the patch of land.

Some people in the town donated money to lay another astroturf wicket in the middle of the field, to turn Kaharlyk CC into Ukraine's first dedicated cricket ground. The pitch and the ground met the ICC's strict playing standards, meaning that if Ukraine became a member one day, the town could host its international games.

The ground was officially opened in 2013, with a match between Kaharlyk CC and an invitational side from Kyiv. The game was arranged for Wayne

Zschech's birthday, which was also the birthday of his team's Ukrainian wicketkeeper. Posters in Ukrainian were put up around the town: 'For the first time in Kaharlyk – the world's second most popular sport. At 12:00 on 8 May there will be an exhibition cricket match. Venue: the cricket ground (next to the wooden houses). A free hot dog for all guests and supporters!'

Even after two decades in Ukraine, Zschech had not lost touch with his Aussie roots. The words on the poster were placed over a picture of England's Jonathan Trott being run out by Simon Katich in an Ashes Test against Australia.

By the time his ground began to host matches, Wayne Zschech had been playing in tournaments in Kyiv for several years. He had become one of the country's most prolific batters – he scored a century the previous summer against the team of English dads – but he was hesitant to bring his Ukrainian cricketers to play in the capital with him.

In Kyiv hostilities would flare up between the Indian-born players. Off the field the men belonged to different social castes and states, and many were business competitors during the week. 'It seemed that that's where the bosses of the different groups would sort out their stuff,' says Zschech. 'It was not an environment that you would bring Ukrainians into.

Australians play hard, but when the umpire puts his finger up, you're out, and it's over.' In Kyiv the feuds could simmer for weeks.

Instead, at home he tried to foster a team in his image. At the beginning his players played in whites, and their nets and matches mirrored the cricket he had played as a child in Hervey Bay.

When he eventually began to take teams from Kaharlyk CC to play in tournaments in Kyiv, it was a chastening experience. 'I would bring my Ukrainians and we were just cannon fodder,' Zschech says. 'We made progress, but we weren't going to win against the best teams. If I had a really good game we were in with a chance, but if I got out early, it was over.'

The boys loved the game, but in the words of their captain, 'it wasn't a lot of fun being punished on a terrible dustbowl of a field.' Before long an inferiority complex set in. The Ukrainians needed belief that they could compete with the Indians. Eventually, after several years of trying, their moment came.

One morning they turned up for a game against a team whose opening batter had scored a brutal century against them the last time they played. This time he didn't score a run. From the first ball of the match he punched a clean cover drive and set off languidly for a single. At mid-off Seryozha Slinko, a small and stocky young man, dived at full stretch to stop the ball, picked himself up, and threw down the stumps at the bowler's end from 20 yards, with the batter well short of the crease.

There was bedlam on the pitch. 'In that couple of seconds, Ukrainian cricket changed,' the pastor beams again. 'Suddenly the Ukrainians were worth something.'

The field in Kaharlyk soon replaced the crumbling Voskhod stadium as Ukrainian cricket's main ground. Teams began to invite themselves to stay with the Zschech family at their church, arriving from far-away Kharkiv as well as Kyiv. On some weekends in the summer the spare rooms had 50 cricketers at a time bunking in them.

There is no way that the Ukrainian team could have intended it, but in time the ground at Kaharlyk became as intimidating a place for the Indians to travel to as the Voskhod stadium in Kyiv had once been for them. The astroturf pitch on the school playing field played like a fast and bouncy Australian wicket: the Ukrainians who learned their cricket with Wayne Zschech had better techniques to bat and bowl on it.

Cricket may have been in the Indians' blood, but they were all brought up on tape-ball games; many of them had never played with a hard ball, or on a proper grass field, until their first match in Kaharlyk. Zschech compares their experience to foreign Test players trying to bat in Perth: 'If everywhere else they're playing in the country bounces low, Indian, this is bouncing high, WACA … in our batting cage and out in the field, the ball would bounce truer and higher, so our guys had some kind of advantage.'

Another advantage the Ukrainians had was how seriously they took their fielding. Zschech tells me about another moment when his team earned some respect, this time thanks to another of his young players, Vlad. 'In one game we had them down 4-20 or something. And these are really good cricket players. Then Hardeep got a short-pitched ball. He square-pulled it right at square-leg; it hits Vlad, and it bounces up and it lands in his hands. It was even more unbelievable than the run-out in Kyiv. He had a massive bruise on his ribs …'

Kaharlyk CC lost far more games than they won, but on their day they could upset the best teams in the country. In June 2015 the Ukrainians caused a shock in the opening match of the Kyiv Cricket League, winning by seven wickets against a Seniors XI whose 161 they chased down in 18 overs.

Playing in all of these games was Yuri Zahurskiy, still batting left-handed with his big County 555. After teaching himself to bat, 'Yura' learned to bowl off-breaks as well and took plenty of wickets for the various teams he played for – often when well-set batters saw his very unorthodox action and became complacent. He was also one of the best fielders in Ukraine, thanks to the same powerful hands that helped him to hit the ball so hard at the crease.

Stories about Yuri Zahurskiy, the gentle giant of Ukrainian cricket, had cropped up so often that I wondered whether I should spoil the legend by trying to contact him. Wayne Zschech also warned me that before the war he had been coming to terms with a personal tragedy, and had thrown himself into humanitarian work as soon as the invasion began. I write Zahurskiy a message but don't expect to hear back from him, until one day a reply comes through: 'No, I don't think you're pressuring me. I myself want to talk about how I started playing cricket. Maybe someone will find it interesting …'

In my head was Zschech's 'fridge of a bloke', with huge hands bruising balls to the boundary. I wasn't expecting Zahurskiy to write about cricket like a complex maths equation to be solved. He clearly took his practice in the nets and the mushroom barn extremely seriously.

'The barn was 6 metres by 30 metres,' he remembers. 'This allowed me to develop the basic techniques for a bowler and batter. The training sessions were long and exhausting, because to play cricket you need particular muscles and reactions, and a lot of other nuances come into the process of the game.' In a converted barn in central Ukraine, a biofuel developer was setting about learning to play cricket with the determination of a first-class player.

Later that day another message comes through: 'After a while I was invited to play for one of the teams in a tournament. This was a new experience, and so I needed to do new analysis. Cricket has special tactics, and intrigue. A player's success depends only on how they have prepared for the game.'

'My first results were very small,' Zahurskiy says of Kaharlyk CC's demoralising first trips up to Kyiv. 'I still had a lot to learn. But my friend and trainer Wayne really motivated me. He could sometimes score over 100 runs in a match. He could also bowl crafty balls at the batter.'

It was the first time I had heard a Ukrainian's perspective on the culture clash between the beginners from Kaharlyk and the ultra-confident Asian-born cricketers from Kharkiv and Kyiv. Zahurskiy echoes his friend and captain, saying that 'because we were the first Ukrainian team, and didn't play very well, often they underestimated us as opponents. In one tournament we were drawn to play against the strongest team at that time, a side called "Istil". When the match began it was obvious that they weren't taking us seriously, and we managed to score a lot of runs. I don't remember how many exactly, but they had a few really nervous moments before they won.'

It could have been that Istil's players weren't bowling seriously because they were sportingly trying to let Kaharlyk have a proper innings and set up an enjoyable chase. It says a lot about the Ukrainian sporting mentality that Zahurskiy would rather have faced their bowlers at full steam.

Still, the South Asians' exuberance again spilled over into something that the Ukrainian players found hard to digest. 'They were so happy with their victory that they were dancing in the stands,' Zahurskiy remembers. 'They and their supporters were that happy that the strongest side had beaten one of the weakest teams.'

On paper it was certainly a David-versus-Goliath match: Istil were the cricket team affiliated to the Istil Group, which was owned by the Donetsk billionaire Mohammad Zahoor. While sides from the capital often wore colourful cricket uniforms with their teams' names and sponsors on, Kaharlyk CC usually took the field in matching blue cotton souvenir t-shirts with Ukraine's national symbol, a yellow trident sign called the *tryzub*, on the front.

I ask Yuri about other interesting and funny moments from his career. When he writes about a dangerous batter jogging through for a single, only for the Ukrainian at mid-off to hit the wickets with one stump to aim at, I realise that he is describing the same run-out, by Seryozha Slinko, that Wayne Zschech had been so emotional about as well. It becomes clear that all the Ukrainians at Kaharlyk CC had tried very hard to get better at cricket, and it had hurt them to be treated as inferior. Zahurskiy adds: 'All the interesting and funny moments came about because other teams underestimated us. That game made our opponents respect us.'

I wanted to hear about his best innings, so I asked him about the moments on a cricket field that have made him most proud. But Ukraine's best cricketer is not one to boast. 'I'm proud to have played cricket with my two sons, Petro and Veniamin. They were also quite good at it. My youngest son Veniamin was on the way to reaching his potential, but he had already achieved quite a lot.'

When I finally get him to talk about his own favourite innings, he still deflects the attention on to his sons. 'Both of them surpassed their father. My record score is 54, and they beat it: Petro's was 56, and Veniamin's was 57. If it wasn't for Covid-19, and then the war, I'm sure they would have scored even more.

My youngest son is in Germany now. And to my great sadness, my eldest son is no longer with us.'

This is the trauma that Yuri has been coping with. His son Petro Zahurskiy, a healthy 28-year-old with the same weightlifter physique as his father, died of pneumonia resulting from Covid-19 in April 2020. 'Petya' was a talented and popular member of Ukraine's cricketing family. In his honour some cricket teams got together in Kaharlyk in the summer of 2020 to play in the Petya Zahurskiy Memorial Cup. A photograph from the day shows a tearful Yuri in a floppy white cricket hat, standing next to the tournament poster with Petya's photo on.

Some months after Yuri tells me about his late son, I realise that I have heard Petya's voice. In the BBC *Test Match Special* segment in 2012 about the English touring side's match in Kyiv, the radio journalist speaks to a Ukrainian player who introduces himself as Peter. In good English, Petya, who would then have been about 20, says that he learned to play cricket with his father, and now also plays with his friends.

Petya laughs when the man from the BBC asks if he is more of a bowler or a batter: 'I don't know! Both are good. I'm learning … I'm always practising batting and bowling. We're working together as a team. It's good, everyone is encouraging each other.'

What did his friends make of cricket? 'They thought that it's croquet – the game with the hammers? So I explained to them what cricket is. After that they were like: "oh, it's baseball!", so I had to explain that no, it's not baseball. But then some of them came to play with us, and they were like: "yeah, this is a cool game!" Maybe my other friends from university will also come and practice with us. I hope so.'

Does cricket have the potential to be as popular in Ukraine as football or ice hockey? 'Sure,' Petya says. 'We're dreaming about that! We're dreaming that it will be really popular; that many people will want to know more about cricket. We need more Ukrainians…'

Petya mentions that Wayne Zschech sends his team cricket videos to help them to learn the game. 'He sends us links online, so me and my father can watch. It's pretty interesting to look how professionals are playing, and to learn from them how to bowl, how to throw the ball, and all this stuff.'

And how about Petya's ambition in cricket? 'I want to hit the ball to a six,' he laughs again. 'My father has done that, and my friend has done that, but I still haven't. I have been Man of the Match, but I still haven't scored a six. I'll keep trying. I'm practising for that.'

Cricket became a big part of the Zahurskiy family, even if playing for Kaharlyk CC could be disheartening, as Zschech had told me. A scorecard from 2013, the year after the *TMS* interview, shows Petya, batting at six, bowled for a first-ball duck against one of the Kyiv teams. Wayne had already been run out for 3; Yuri, at seven, made 12 from 18 balls.

Through the death of a son, and the war that has shattered the Chernihiv region where he was born, the senior Zahurskiy hasn't put away his County 555. 'I'm going to turn 55 this year,' he says. 'But I still dream of playing cricket again. This game has given me a lot of friends, emotions, excitement. And the desire to play more and more.'

If Yuri never plays another innings, then he retires with a special place in European sport. His innings of 54 came in the Friends' Cup in Kyiv in 2021, at the age of 53. In any country in the world, a cricketer who can score a half-century in a competitive hard-ball match, against bowlers raised on the Asian subcontinent, is a serious player. That Yuri Zahurskiy made so many runs having held a cricket bat for the first time in his forties, teaching himself to bat in rural Ukraine after discovering the game at a barbecue, makes his career even more incredible.

Since the start of 2022 he has put his strength and enormous heart to more important use. The moment the invasion began, the people living in Ukraine had no other thoughts besides keeping their loved ones safe. In the last week of February Yuri Zahurskiy went one step further, volunteering to help people escape from the towns outside Kyiv, where Russian soldiers were torturing and killing ordinary civilians.

'In the first days of the war a lot of people called me and asked for help. It was friends, acquaintances, and people I didn't know, who had heard that I was involved in evacuating people. While I was getting people out of Kyiv I was constantly thinking about my family. Since 2020 my family and I had been suffering from the awful loss of my eldest son. I didn't even want to think that I could lose someone else in my family. I asked my family to leave Ukraine and go to Europe, but they didn't want to leave me on my own.

'On the second day of the war I managed to convince them to leave. They went in the car of my daughter-in-law, Maryna. I filled up their tank with petrol and gave them some canisters so that they could get over the country's border, because there was no petrol in the fuel stations. After that I was calmer, knowing that they were safe.

'It took them four days to travel the 650km (400 miles) to the border. The roads were full of refugees trying to escape from the war.

'My car was a Volkswagen Sharan. It could fit seven passengers inside, but then there was no room for their belongings. More and more people were calling me. A lot of people were asking me to evacuate them from Bucha. There were a lot of people trapped there, and among them were a lot of children.' In several trips into Bucha, Zahurskiy rescued several people from a town where marauding Russian conscripts were indiscriminately killing peaceful residents.

'On March 2nd I asked someone I knew to use his Toyota minibus, which could fit 12 people inside. God helped me to get people out.

'The town of Bucha had already been attacked several times by Russian troops. At Ukrainian checkpoints they tried to stop me going any further. I had to explain that I had to collect the children there. They said that I was mad and let me through.

'The next day I needed to go for more people, but the owner of the minibus wouldn't give it to me anymore. I went in my Volkswagen instead.

'As I arrived in Bucha I saw military vehicles and another checkpoint. I thought it was our Ukrainian army, but they opened fire on me with machine guns, and my vehicle cut out in the middle of the road. It was one of the Russian army's sabotage groups; three armoured reconnaissance and patrol vehicles. I went into shock for a time, but then I quickly realised that they were Russian orcs.'

In an example of the dark and defiant humour that Ukrainians have showed since the first days of the war, orcs, the malevolent breed of human-like monsters in J.R.R Tolkien's *Lord of the Rings*, is the name they use for the invading Russian soldiers.

'I wanted to jump out of the vehicle and hide somewhere,' Zahurskiy continues, 'but the side of the road was very wide, and bullets were still flying there. I decided to stay in my vehicle, so that they would think that they had hit me. I sat and prayed to God. I said goodbye to life in this world, and asked to be forgiven for my sins. I waited for one more round of machine gun fire. But my God decided to keep me alive.

'Some time later they left. I managed not to panic. After I assessed the situation I got out of my vehicle. People began to walk towards me; they had been in various hiding places and had seen what happened to me. They all asked me if I was alive. I left my vehicle on the road and went on foot back to where I had come from.'

After recuperating at home in Kaharlyk for a little while, Yuri Zahurskiy was soon working in the war zone again. By April he was bringing food and other supplies to villages that had been cut off from the rest of the country.

Meanwhile, Zschech and his wife and children had left Kaharlyk, and flown to the pastor's childhood home on Australia's east coast. But they weren't leaving Ukraine behind: the family were going on a fundraising mission to raise money for the Ukrainian communities trapped in the war zone. The Christian organisation that the Zschechs are a part of, Operation Mobilisation, needed to keep buying food and arranging drop-offs, so that Zahurskiy and their other partners could deliver aid parcels to the towns for as long as they could.

In May the Zschechs returned to Ukraine, and Wayne and his close friend Yuri spent the summer of 2022 delivering humanitarian aid to frontline towns in their minivan. They were able to keep people alive in places like Borodyanka outside Kyiv, where about three-quarters of the buildings were destroyed by aerial bombing, and dozens of people were killed.

Back in Kaharlyk, Olha Zschech prepared some rooms in their church, where the cricketers used to sleep during tournaments, for Ukrainian families who have been forced to leave their homes in other parts of the country. These days when the congregation of Calvary Chapel see new people in the church before a Sunday service, they understand what has brought them there.

Chapter Four

DEEP COVER

IT IS a warm, late February morning in Rajkot, in the western Indian state of Gujarat. The groundsmen at the Saurashtra Cricket Association Stadium are preparing for the start of a four-day fixture in the Ranji Trophy, the country's storied first-class competition.

Gujarat's opponents this week are Kerala, a strong team from the south-west tip of the country. In their opening match Kerala had trounced Meghalaya – the tiny, hilly state in the far north-west of India – by an innings and were the favourites to progress from Group A to reach the Ranji quarter-finals.

Gujarat had lost to a good Madhya Pradesh side the week before and had some ground to catch up. At the toss, Kerala's captain Sachin Baby calls correctly and puts Gujarat in to bat.

The first hour belongs to Kerala. When their opening bowler Basil Thampi – like his captain, a recent India A player – traps the Gujarat No. 4 Manprit Juneja in front for 3, the home side are 33/4.

As the wickets fall in Rajkot, Baby and Thampi's former team-mate Faisal Kassim, 4,000km (2,500 miles) away in Kharkiv, is running to a bomb shelter.

Kassim was now in his fifth year as a medical student in Ukraine, but as a teenager he had spent five years as a pace bowler at the Kerala Cricket Association's academy in Kochi. He grew up playing alongside Thampi and Baby for the state's junior teams. The young Faisal had also played cricket with Sanju Samson, the captain of Rajasthan Royals in the IPL, who now plays one-day cricket for India.

Kassim dreamed of playing first-class cricket for Kerala, and for a while a place in their Ranji Trophy side was his for the taking. In 2015 he was part of the Kerala under-16 team that played in the Vijay Merchant Trophy, a prestigious month-long tournament for India's best schoolboy cricketers. Matches in the competition are played over four innings, and news of big scores and X-factor bowlers quickly travels across India. Kassim was selected for three of Kerala's five games in Hyderabad; he took a couple of wickets opening the bowling, and ended the tournament with an innings of 36 against Goa.

Three years later a spinal cord injury brought his dream to a sudden end. No longer able to play competitive cricket, his parents insisted that he focus on his studies. One of his distant cousins was already studying in Ukraine, so in 2018 Kassim moved to the Black Sea city of Odesa, to enrol at the city's medical university.

Kassim soon found out that there was some cricket in Kyiv. Still able to bowl a few overs a week without pain, at weekends he took a bus to the capital, a round trip of 14 hours and almost 1,000km (620 miles), to play in an eight-team league that Thamarai Pandian was running. The players who were available the evening before the matches would get together to train under floodlights on one of Kyiv's amateur football pitches.

While playing in the games in Kyiv he got to know Hardeep Singh, the boss of Ukrainian cricket, who told him about the busy cricket scene in Kharkiv. Singh persuaded Kassim to leave Odesa, and switch to one of the degrees that his company offered at Kharkiv National Medical University. Faisal was living in one of Singh's dorms in the north of the city, on Liudviha Svobody Avenue, when the bombings started in February 2022.

His three years in Kharkiv were consumed by cricket. Kassim and his course-mates ended up spending almost as much time playing T20 matches on the university's football pitches as they did in lectures.

Naturally for a group where most of the students were from India, cricket culture in Kharkiv was modelled on the IPL. The league had 16 teams. Squads were usually made up of players from the same Indian state, but some of the campus's tech-savvy students organised an online auction, which allowed students to be traded between teams. These auctions made sure that every team had enough batters and bowlers, and everyone who wanted to play got a proper game.

Kassim soon stood out as one of the best cricketers in Kharkiv. Each season his injured spine got stronger, and his pace gradually returned. While behind the scenes Thamarai Pandian and Hardeep Singh were doing the paperwork that would allow Ukraine to join the ICC, they were lining up Faisal Kassim to take the new ball for its men's national team.

It isn't hard to see why Hardeep Singh was so keen to look after the young pacer: Singh himself had ended up studying in Ukraine after a spinal injury ended his own dreams of professional cricket. And as he began to think about entering teams into ICC tournaments, he could imagine what the 21-year-old Kassim, who was once timed at 135kph (84 mph) at the Kerala academy in Kochi, would do to European top orders as soon as he was given a chance.

The standard of cricket in Kharkiv was very mixed, but thanks to the people who organised the leagues, everyone who played there was pampered like an IPL star. The students turning out for teams like the Southern Scorpions, Black Panthers or International Villagers on weekday evenings played in coloured uniforms sponsored by local companies, and batted with expensive bats and pads imported from India.

Between innings the players were treated to meals from Singh's new restaurant, India Palace. His businesses had made him a millionaire several times over, and there were whispers in the dorms that he spent 15% of the money he made on their cricket. Behind the scenes, the Ukrayinska Federatsiya Kriketu, while still unrecognised by the ICC, employed a media manager, and even an operations team.

The league's other sponsors made sure that there was money in it for the players: the best bowler and batter every match would be handed $100 in cash, and there was usually a prize for the longest six as well. As much as some of the students needed the money, they never kept any of the prizes for themselves: the cash would always be spent on buying meals for their team-mates after the games.

And so it came to be that in 2019, while his childhood friend KM Asif had signed an INR 40 lakh ($55,000) IPL contract as a pace bowler with the Chennai Super Kings, Faisal Kassim was bowling for biryani money for the BobTrade Super Kings.

Kassim now lives in Tbilisi, Georgia. But speaking from his new home, he shows no sadness about missing his chance to turn professional in India. If anything, his eyes shine brighter when talking about playing cricket in Ukraine. He was one of the sleepy cricketers who the churchgoers of Kaharlyk had disturbed all those years ago. 'It was so fun,' he says on a video call. 'We played for eight days straight and we all stayed together. We made a barbecue at the ground after matches, and we all sat together and talked. Those moments are still blissful to me.'

Kassim is in Tbilisi because that is where the students on BobTrade courses were transferred to after the Russian army invaded Kharkiv. He would later tell me about how he spent eight days in a bomb shelter when the war began, and how he managed to get out of Ukraine.

As traumatic as his year has been, the cricket matches in Ukraine are still etched into his memory. In one match, he tells me, he was on strike with three balls of the final over remaining, and 13 runs still needed for his team to win. The situation was hopeless: the bowler running in was a wily medium-pacer who was also being looked at for the national team. But Kassim had his eye in. Two sixes and a single later, his team-mates were running towards him to mob him on the outfield.

That night was Eid ul Fitr, the evening that marks the end of Ramadan. Faisal and the campus's other Muslim students got together for a special dinner in the room of his distant cousin, Abdul Vahab, who Kassim had joined in Ukraine. But the host barely said a word to any of his guests all night. He was especially quiet with Faisal: it was Abdul Vahab's medium pace that his cousin had dispatched for two sixes to win the match earlier that day.

Agonising last overs became a theme in the Kharkiv leagues. Once Kassim's team was playing in a semi-final where his team needed 31 from the last six balls. Eight of their batters were already out, including Faisal. The opposition captain, sensing that his team had already won, threw the ball to a new player, Pandey ('Happy Pandey' to his friends), who no one had seen bowl before. The batter on Kassim's team proceeded to smash his first four balls for six; he then hit a four, to leave the stunned Pandey with only three runs to defend off the last ball of the match. The final hit was caught on the boundary at long-on: the catch left Kassim's team centimetres short of a place in the final, and made Pandey much more happy than he had been a moment before.

The raucous games caught the attention of other students on the campus, and a few Ukrainians began to join in. Kassim describes how 'a lot of teachers who hadn't seen cricket before came to watch us, and we taught them to play. We gave cricket classes to Ukrainian students too.' One April on World Sports Day some of the students put on a cricket workshop in the centre of Kharkiv.

While Hardeep Singh was treating his students like IPL stars, it was only fair that they trained like them. In January 2022 Faisal and Abdul Vahab began to call the campus's standout cricketers for compulsory evening nets on their university's indoor basketball court. The young men had a huge motivation to improve over the winter: Ukraine had been invited to send a team to the high-profile Mediterranean Cricket League (MCL) – a competition that was actually held in Croatia, on the Adriatic Sea – the following July.

Although it isn't an ICC event, the MCL is spoken of as the most professionally organised T20 tournament in mainland Europe. The players weren't keen on walking home from training in the dark, minus-20 cold and through shin-deep snow, but as Kassim explains: 'We all knew that if you don't practice in winter, it's very hard to play in summer.'

The MCL was created by the Croatian Cricket Federation, an Associate ICC member, to bring together the strongest and most ambitious club teams from all corners of Europe. Past finalists have included the champions of Estonia, Saaremaa Kriketiklubi, and the Romanian Bears. The competition is also open to touring sides from traditional cricketing countries. These sides sometimes turn up in Croatia with former Test players in their ranks: one past team from India had Abey Kuruvilla playing for them, and an English club once brought Darren Maddy.

The ICC had confirmed that Ukraine's membership would be finalised by the time the MCL began, so the tournament would be the first time that the country's best players would take the field together as a recognised national team.

And in 2022 the visiting teams would be coming up against even bigger fish than Maddy and Kuruvilla. Faisal Kassim and Abdul Vahab would soon be at the top of their marks running in at Simon Katich, the competition's ambassador. Yuri Zahurskiy and Wayne Zschech would be taking guard against Brad Hogg, playing for an Australian touring team.

Even if the two Australians had been retired for a few years, they would be by far the best opponents that the players from Ukraine had ever played against. Katich finished his career with 58 first-class centuries, 10 of them in Test matches. The left-arm wrist-spinner Hogg took over 150 wickets in one-day internationals.

On the basketball court and in the university dorms that winter, excitement was growing. A cricket squad wearing Ukrainian yellow and blue would soon be travelling abroad to an international cup. Then the bombings began.

Rumours that Russia was planning to invade grew louder in the last months of 2021. India's embassy in Ukraine advised its citizens living in the country to return home; but in turn, the staff at the universities in Kharkiv told the students that the rumours were false. Some of Kassim's classmates flew back to India at the beginning of 2022, but he and his cousin Abdul Vahab chose to stay.

Diplomats at the Indian embassy received intelligence that the invasion would begin on 14 February. When that week ended with the Russian army still camped on its own side of the border, the campus at Kharkiv Medical University began to relax. Faisal Kassim stayed up past midnight on the night of the 23rd looking at flights for a holiday to Dubai in the spring.

He was awoken the next morning by the sounds of his dorm in panic. He tells me: 'At 4:40am my room-mates knocked on my door and said there were strange sounds and lights outside, and I should come fast. I told him: "Bro, you're dreaming, just go back to sleep." But then my phone started ringing. My brother [Abdul Vahab] told me that the bombing had started. They had bombed Kyiv airport, and Kharkiv airport was closed.'

The Indian diplomats had been right about the invasion, just wrong about when it would happen. 'I looked through my window and I could see tanks going fast through the street,' Kassim continues. 'At that moment I froze. My family called. All my friends called. My phone was continuously ringing. The building was shaking. My body went cold.'

There was no time to think. Kassim ran to the nearest supermarket to buy some food and water, then ran up to Abdul Vahab's apartment. At 10am he got a call from Hardeep Singh, who ordered him to go to another dorm building, on Nauki Avenue, where 300 other Indian students were living. They were first-year students, boys and girls of 18 or 19, who had only arrived in Ukraine two weeks earlier. Singh sent Kassim, who had been in Ukraine for four years, was older and spoke Ukraine's languages, to try to keep them safe.

Singh ordered all the students to go down into the building's basement. The cellars beneath housing blocks in Ukraine are often fortified to withstand bomb blasts; they exist as de facto bomb shelters. But still the teenagers had no idea how serious the situation was: when Kassim told them to run outside and buy supplies, some of them came back with small bottles of Coke and crisps.

But as Russian tanks continued to grind through the streets, and the sound of missiles grew louder, the reality of what was happening soon hit them all. Singh sent instructions to switch off all the lights in the building, as by now it was clear that the Russian artillery was targeting places where ordinary civilians lived.

On the night of 24 February the temperature in Kharkiv fell to eight degrees below zero. There was no heating in the basement, and there were no windows. Put in charge of the shelter, Kassim had to make sure that everybody got some sleep. Most of the boys and girls lay on the bare and freezing floor, cuddling each other for warmth. Others closed their eyes while sitting down on the stairs. When the 300 course-mates had each found a place to spend the night, Kassim lay down on his yoga mat and tried to sleep as well.

Not everyone living in the dorm at that time was Indian; Hardeep Singh also rented out some of the rooms to the public. The day the invasion began, the building's residents included eight Russian women, who found themselves in the basement hiding for their lives from their own country's army.

In Rajkot the next day, Friday 25th, Gujarat rallied to score 388 in their first innings. Basil Thampi took some lower-order wickets for Kerala, to finish with the colourful figures of 4-118 from his 19.1 overs. Meanwhile, Faisal Kassim spent the morning cleaning the four toilets on the ground floor of the building. He then ran back up to the dorm rooms to cook meals for everyone, using whatever food he could find.

On the fourth day of the shelling, Sunday 27th, Kerala completed an eight-wicket victory. Sachin Baby added 62 to his first-innings 53 to anchor a chase of 214. A few hours later in Kharkiv, a message reached the students that one of their course-mates had been killed. Naveen Shekharappa Gyanagoudar, from the state of Karnataka, was 21 and in his fourth year at Kharkiv National Medical University. It appears that he was shot dead while running outside his own dorm building to fill up a water bottle.

No one in the cold basement on Nauki Avenue had any doubt now that they were in a war zone. 'We were all terrified,' Kassim says. 'If a missile landed on our building we would be dead also. It was the moment we realised that maybe we were at the end.'

The young doctor sensed that his compatriots were struggling mentally. But his days bowling at the cricket academy in Kochi had taught him never to give up; the spinal injury he suffered at 17 happened at the end of a 23-over spell. Kassim took it upon himself to lift their spirits, forcing them to sing songs and play games. The students also kept their brains switched on by concocting plans on how they could all escape from Ukraine together.

By the eighth day in the basement their food had almost run out. It was time to try one of the plans they had made. They decided to try to get to the city's central train station and catch a train to Poland. But with explosions still being heard – and felt – outside it wasn't safe to walk, and there were no taxis or buses on the streets. The metro system had shut down so that the stations could serve as bomb shelters. The only thing the boys and girls could do was run to the closest metro station and walk through the underground tunnels until they reached the train terminal.

The group hurried to Botanichnyi Sad metro, next to the city's botanical gardens. They jumped the barriers and walked down the escalators into the platforms. Then they walked 13 kilometres through the metro tunnels; several hours later they all arrived, starving and filthy, at the metro next to Kharkiv's central station.

Outside the station the city was in hysteria. The group still had to reach the train station platforms through a mass of screaming people. 'All the students were panicking,' Kassim remembers. 'We could hear the sound of shelling and firing. The [metro] building was shaking all the time; the glass broke from the blasts. Somehow we reached the railway station. But there were around 20,000 people waiting for a train. We jumped over the track to get on to a train.'

Policemen tried to stop men of fighting age from boarding the trains, even those who were clearly in a group of foreign nationals. Amid the hysteria they even threw punches at Faisal and his course-mates as they tried to climb into a carriage.

Faisal and about 70 other students managed to force themselves on to one train headed for the city of Lviv in Ukraine's west, close to the border with Poland. For most of the 16 hours, everyone in the carriages had to stand up. 'The journey was hell,' Kassim says. 'There wasn't even a place to sit on the floor.'

He shouted that he was a trainee doctor, who could attend to any of the passengers who were in pain or distress; but the train was so packed with bodies that when someone in the same carriage called for him, it took him an hour to reach them.

Kassim was only 21 when he guided his fellow students from the basement to the train station, but he had long been a good man to have by your side in a crisis. In the Vijay Merchant Trophy as a 15-year-old he made his biggest innings, the 36 against Goa, through the pain of a torn abdominal muscle. Batting at number 11 in the order, he lasted 104 balls to help Kerala to add 80 for the last wicket. After being outclassed by all of their other opponents, the partnership against Goa would eventually secure Kerala a first-innings lead, and a winning draw.

When the young men and women arrived in Lviv the next day they had to wait for a bus to take them to the border with Poland. Traumatised by the stress of spending more than a week in the underground shelter, every loud noise sent fear through the whole group.

Faisal Kassim stayed on the Ukrainian side of the border for two days, helping and translating for his compatriots until they could get across to Poland safely. He had become the point of contact for the parents of the younger students and was so overwhelmed updating 60 families in India about what was happening that he barely managed to speak with his own. As soon as he could leave Lviv he went to a town in Poland; he thinks it was Rzeszów, but isn't sure.

He spent three days in a hostel there. Only then could he check in with his cricketer friends across Ukraine. Mercifully, no one had suffered any physical injuries, although all were mentally exhausted by what they were being forced to go through.

In the second week of March Faisal flew from Warsaw to Delhi. There, lodging at the city's Kerala House, he changed out of the one set of clothes he had been wearing since entering the dorm basement in Kharkiv. He ate some fresh food for the first time in over a week. 'The experience of those 10 days of my life – there are not enough words to explain my emotions,' Kassim says, smiling, from Georgia.

At the same time as Ukraine's star bowler was waking up to Russian tanks crunching underneath his window, another important figure in Ukrainian cricket was watching Russian bombs fall in his neighbourhood. Binil Zachariah had also come to Kharkiv from Kerala, to study for an aerospace engineering degree at Kharkiv Aviation Institute. After completing his course in 2016, Hardeep Singh gave him a job as a graphic designer at BobTrade Education Group, allowing him to stay in Ukraine with his wife, Yulia, and their young daughter Emily. Singh also brought Binil – or 'Zack', as everyone in Ukraine knew him – into the Ukraine cricket family, as its media manager.

As the Ukraine Cricket Federation set its sights on operating as an ICC member, Zack developed its bilingual website, designed the teams' jerseys, and took photographs (and made slick drone videos) at its tournaments. He was also one of the few people entrusted with the paperwork for Ukraine's membership application.

'Every time we had cricket, it was like a carnival,' Zack writes when I send him a message in August 2022, six months into the invasion. 'On three or four days every month, at weekends, we were celebrating cricket. [With about] 50% of the cricketers being medical students, with all the academic stress they had, cricket was equal to having a drink after a hectic day at work.

'The funny thing is that although they were students, some of them took cricket much more seriously than their studies. They even used to skip their classes to attend our practice sessions and tournaments all over Ukraine.'

While Faisal Kassim and most of Kharkiv's other Indians lived in dorms near the centre of the city, Zack, Yulia and five-year-old Emily rented their own apartment. They lived in the eastern district of Saltivka, only 15km (9 miles) away from the border with Russia. As we speak by video call a year into the war, the Zachariah family are now in Canada, having settled in the city of Calgary. All three survived a harrowing journey to get there.

'I woke up from all these sounds outside,' Zack says of the morning of 24 February. 'First I was thinking it's some kind of birthday celebration; somebody enjoying their night. But then I understood it's not the firecrackers that I usually heard. Fireworks always used to come from the nearest park, but this sound came from all over. I knew that they were bombs, and that they [the Russians] didn't know where they were aiming.

'I knew it was dangerous for us. I knew that I could not spend one more minute at home – the next bomb could hit us. So I told my wife to get up, and got my daughter ready. I only had three backpacks. I grabbed everything I could: my wallet, my phone, my laptop, a few other things, and some food for my daughter. I couldn't even take any of my clothes.'

Having lived in Kharkiv for ten years, Zack knew that the metro stations in the country's cities were built to withstand bombs, even small nuclear bombs. The family rushed to their nearest station, Heroyiv Pratsi; the name means 'Heroes of Labour', in honour of the

Soviet Russian and Ukrainian workers who built the city together in the last century. Before they went underground, the couple arranged for their landlord to come to their apartment to save the family's cat, Muthu, who they couldn't take with them.

The metro trains had stopped running, as shellshocked Ukrainians fled underground to shelter from the bombs. But the trains began moving again in the late morning, to let people escape from the edges of the city.

Zack decided to take his family into the centre. He reasoned that if the Russian army was planning on occupying Kharkiv, it would not destroy all of it, and would spare the central parts of the city from shelling. They travelled seven stops west to reach Naukova metro station. In the melee on the platforms Zack could see small groups of his countrymen – fellow cricketers from the nearby medical school.

He managed to catch a few words with some of them. He recalls: 'Almost all the cricketers in Kharkiv were making sure that all their friends and loved ones were safe, and helping each other to get out of the war zone as soon as possible. Abdul Vahab and Swadhin [Mohapatra, also part of the cricket federation's 'operations' team] were leading the evacuation plans. But we all lost some of our friends in the invasion. I had better say "invasion", not war, because as you know, it is totally one-sided.'

As the family sat on the metro platform, they had no idea how long they would be there for. In the end it would be 11 days before they could leave.

Almost everyone in the metro was resigned to defeat. The consensus among the hundreds of Kharkiv residents camped on the platforms was that the city would fall under Russian control in four or five days. As the days went by, Zack's life revolved around waiting for a turn to charge his phone, so that he and Yulia could keep in touch with their families.

At night they lay down on the platforms, but adrenaline, and the painful cold, stopped them from sleeping. Even at their home in Saltivka, Emily was afraid of the dark; nights on the floor of the station were agony for her.

Resistance by Ukrainian forces meant that the city held out for longer than five days. But Zack was wrong to think that they would be safer in the centre. On 2 March, the Zachariah family's seventh day in Naukova station, Russian missiles began to fall overhead.

Often when people tried to go up the escalators and outside to look for food, they were forced back underground by the sound of shelling. It was then that Zack began to contemplate death – a thought being shared in those same hours by Faisal Kassim across the city, and Kobus Olivier in Kyiv. 'We heard shelling nearby,' Zack says. 'It was so loud that the ground was shaking. We didn't know if we would be alive the next day. When is it going to happen, that was what we were waiting for.'

When the explosions reached the centre of Kharkiv, Emily and some of the other children living on the platforms of Naukova metro were taken into a cell, deeper inside the station, where it was safer. Some of the policemen guarding the station broke into a nearby McDonald's and carried some bread down to the shelter, so that the people camping on the platforms at Naukova would not need to go above ground themselves to look for food.

Zack had no doubt that this was not a 'special military operation', as the invasion was being called in Russia, but a campaign of indiscriminate bombing. He was able to exchange messages with Hardeep Singh, who was using his contacts in India's diplomatic corps to relay information to his staff and students. 'Indian diplomats got information from the Russian parliament that Putin is going crazy, and is trying to destroy everything,' he grimaces. As soon as he heard this, he understood that his family would never see their home in Saltivka again.

'We got some information that Russia was going to make it even worse,' he says. 'So the best thing to do was leave the country.' But after 11 days in the metro station they barely had strength to walk. Somehow, they put together enough steps to emerge from the platform.

'We had some courage. No, not courage: it was …' He can't find the word in English, so he switches to the Russian that he has always spoken at home with Yulia. 'It was … *pofig* ("I don't care anymore"). Without that mindset, I don't think we would have come out of the station.'

Like his good friend Faisal Kassim and his group of students, Zack took his family to the train station. But by this time all men of fighting age were being stopped from boarding the carriages. Zack knew that if he was separated from Yulia and Emily he might never see them again.

Just as he was losing hope, another message came through from Hardeep Singh. He had arranged for three buses to take as many BobTrade students and staff as possible to Lviv. Zack jumped on a bus with his wife and daughter. From Lviv they travelled in a car to the border with Poland. The family arrived in Warsaw on 5 March, where they stayed for a few months before flying to Canada.

Of course not all of the Indian students who found themselves trapped in Kharkiv at the start of the invasion were interested in cricket. But the friendships formed between those who did play helped the young men and women to survive in their shelters. 'Cricket created a very strong bond between us,' Zack tells me. 'We had WhatsApp groups for all the cricketers; we used to message each other, and tried to make sure that we were all safe during those terrifying days.

'It took almost 20 days from 24 February to get all of us out of Kharkiv. I can't thank Mr Hardeep Singh enough for all the patience he had, even when people were losing their minds, and running around trying to save their own lives. He was the one who led all of us to safety. He made sure that all of us were out before he left Ukraine.'

Zack mentions that although all of the Indian students were offered places on the buses that would take them close to the Polish border, some of the cricketers chose to stay in Kharkiv, to help their course-mates, of all nationalities, to get to safety. Of Saltivka, his home for many years, he says: 'That place is awful now. I'm sure that if we had stayed there, we wouldn't be alive by now.'

Near the end of our call, Emily strolls into the frame to rest her head on her father's shoulder. I wait until she is out of earshot before asking Zack who is to blame for this war, which has torn their and tens of millions of other lives to pieces.

It takes him a second to reply: 'Putin. For sure. Putin, that's it. Putin.

'I get emotional when I see photos from Ukraine on my phone. My family, cricket … now it's a lost chapter in my life. Before the war I had a totally different vision of Putin. But since the war started, I hate him.'

On 2 March 2022, while millions of people in Ukraine were hiding for their lives, the United Nations General Assembly adopted a resolution demanding that Russia withdraw its forces and abide by international law. Of the 146 countries to vote, 141 supported the resolution. The five countries to vote against it were Russia, Belarus, North Korea, Eritrea and Syria.

A little over a year later, in March 2023, the International Criminal Court in The Hague issued an arrest warrant for Vladimir Putin. The court concluded that there were reasonable grounds to believe that in the first year of the war the Russian president was responsible for the unlawful deportation of several thousand Ukrainian children to Russia – an act that constitutes a war crime. There are reports that many of these children were sent to "re-education" camps, thousands of kilometres from their families in Ukraine.

Many people, however, do not lay the blame for what is happening in Ukraine with Putin. Moscow's propaganda about the war – that its military is freeing Russians from persecution by 'Nazis', and that Russia is defending itself against threats from the western world – are supported by many, in Europe and beyond. One of them is Kobus Olivier.

In the months after he arrived in Croatia the South African teacher gave many interviews about his escape from Kyiv. Olivier reached out to so many types of media that a talk with the American Scott Ritter, a controversial media figure whose opinions often echo Russian disinformation, might not have meant anything on its own.

But on social media Olivier himself shared Russia's conspiracies, tweeting about 'the Zelenskyy Nazi regime' and 'churches that Zelenskyy and the Neo Nazis [sic] are destroying'. During 2023 he reposted hundreds of messages supporting the invasion. Over a thousand pro-Russia 'likes' included several videos of Putin speeches, and one photograph with the caption 'Donetsk under Ukrainian terror'.

In his interviews Olivier spoke against the suffering that people were being put through. But the spokesperson for Ukrainian cricket, the old Moscow ambassador's nephew, thought that Ukrainians were bringing the bombings upon themselves.

Chapter Five

FIRST ELEVENS

HE MAY have become a millionaire in Ukraine, but
for Hardeep Singh the country was only a back-up
plan. One of the generation of Indian boys inspired by
Kapil Dev's team that won the 1983 World Cup, as a
child he dreamed of being a cricketer. His idols were
Mohinder Amarnath and Madan Lal, the players from
that side that came from his home state of Punjab. He
got closer than most to living that dream. As a teenager
in Jalandhar at the end of the 1980s Singh was on the
way to becoming the next Lal, at least when it came to
his seam bowling.

By the age of 17 he was playing in Punjab's under-19
squad, just a step away from the Ranji Trophy. Before
that he was an eye-catching under-16 cricketer in Pune,
the city outside Mumbai where his father was serving
in the Indian army. In schools cricket he played against

Sharadashram Vidyamandir School in Mumbai, where the young Hardeep Singh must have bowled at Sachin Tendulkar.

In the summer of 2022 we meet in London, where he is having a short break with his wife and daughter. After evacuating the last of his BobTrade students and staff from Kharkiv in March he moved his family to Dubai, where he has been picking up the pieces of his life. In a lobby at his hotel in Westminster the quietly-spoken Singh, approaching his 50th birthday, tells me how he had brought cricket to Ukraine almost 30 years ago.

'I used to play a lot of cricket in India, at certain levels,' he begins. 'But when I was 17 I got a serious back injury, and I had to leave the professional teams. In those times we didn't have medications, physiotherapy, etc. – it was all very raw in India at that time.'

As his future as a professional cricketer was taken away, not all the pain that Singh had to cope with was physical. 'Due to my back injury you could say I went into a depression,' he says. 'I just wanted to move away from cricket.'

Moving away from cricket meant moving away from India. In the winter of 1993 he moved to Kharkiv to study at an aviation institute. It was a big step for a 20-year-old from Punjab, but in the grand scheme of things Hardeep wasn't going too far off the beaten path.

Delhi was always a firm ally of the Soviet Union, and universities in the USSR were full of Indian students on engineering courses. Even after the empire was split into 15 independent republics, institutes in big former Soviet cities, like Kharkiv, had good reputations in South Asia.

Like his eventual deputy Kobus Olivier, part of Singh's reason for moving to Ukraine was to get as far away from cricket as possible. And like Olivier, it didn't take long for the cricket bug to find him again. Feeling homesick one day, the idea came to him to play some cricket with some of his compatriots. The students would sneak on to the parks dotted around Kharkiv in the evenings, after the footballers had left.

Without bats or any other equipment, Singh had to improvise. 'I asked a carpenter to make us some bats,' he says matter-of-factly. 'We took a tennis ball and started playing. And then when I next went to India I got some bats. We started slowly like this. It was all with tennis balls. But then some Pakistani students came to Kharkiv; they were into tape-ball cricket, where you put tape over a tennis ball. We used to play with those, because the balls travel faster. You feel like you're playing normal cricket.'

In the early days the cricketers tried playing a few games with a baseball, but it was too harsh on their hands. The young men couldn't afford to be too reckless, with assignments to write at night after they came home from the parks.

When he completed his degree in 1995, instead of going back to Punjab to follow his father into the army, Singh stayed in Kharkiv. That summer he started a business importing goods from Turkey and selling them around the Donbas region. He spent any free time he had playing cricket.

Hardeep Singh hadn't made it as a professional cricketer, but from nothing he had arranged the first few cricket matches in Ukraine. In the middle of the 1990s he was probably earning more money from his Turkish import business than his friends from the Punjab youth team were for playing in the Ranji Trophy.

Nevertheless, at the beginning cricket culture, like most things in eastern Ukraine in the 1990s, was a very rugged affair. By 1995 Singh and his course-mates were still playing ad hoc tape-ball games in public parks. But he never missed an opportunity to make their matches more fun. 'It was a problem that we couldn't find a proper ground, with a proper pitch, so I brought a matting wicket from India. I paid the excess weight charge and brought it on the flight myself.'

His friends were happy to bat and bowl wherever there was space; but Hardeep Singh, with the lush grounds of Punjab and Pune still in his mind, was fastidious in finding places where there were no holes. The raucous games usually attracted an audience. Singh remembers that 'Ukrainians used to come and watch. They used to ask to try to play. They told us that they have their own similar game, called lapta.'

Until tennis player Elina Svitolina's net in Brisbane, whenever Ukrainians watched cricket for the first time they usually made an association with the old Slavic bat-and-ball game lapta. Lapta was invented long enough ago for 17th-century Tsar Peter I to have made his soldiers play it to keep fit. It was played in villages in parts of the Soviet empire and was a popular pastime in some places in Eurasia into the 20th century, although it is now almost extinct. Many people in Ukraine today have heard of it, even if almost no one has played it themselves.

Played with a tennis ball in the last few decades, on an outfield the size of a field hockey pitch, to the untrained eye lapta looks more like handball or touch rugby than cricket. But there are similarities. Lapta innings begin with a player whacking the ball into the outfield with a wooden paddle that looks exactly like a flat cricket bat. Teams score points by running from one end of the pitch to the other and back again, throwing the ball between themselves as they run. While this is happening, the players on the other team try to stop them by tagging them.

Perhaps even more similar to cricket is an old game called hilka, where players hit a soft ball into a field with a bat, and fielders try to get them out by fetching the ball and throwing it at them. Hilka was thought up in Lviv at the start of the 20th century, but it can't really be said to be a Ukrainian invention: it is almost completely identical to the older English game of rounders.

It's fair to say that lapta and hilka are more genteel hobbies than tape-ball cricket. As the frenetic games appeared in a few places around Kharkiv, not all Ukrainians were curious to get closer to this new sport. 'We played cricket in public spaces, with buildings all around,' Hardeep Singh continues. 'So we had to explain to new players that you can't shout, because if we started shouting people would call the police. If the bowlers appealed, they could only use their hands.'

Cricket in Kharkiv really started to grow after 1995, when Singh set up the BobTrade Education Group. More students in the city meant more cricketers, and more income meant more money to spend on arranging practice sessions and matches. As it had been for Singh when he was a student, cricket became a way for the young men and women to stave off homesickness. The university dorms that he owned began to echo with the sound of tennis balls flying down the corridors.

Every weekend during the summer months he would organise three or four 20-over matches a day. Often these were played on a matting wicket laid in the middle of one of the universities' football pitches; usually Hardeep would lay on an Indian buffet for the players, and for the Ukrainians who came to watch. The buffet came from another of his business ventures in the city: his first restaurant, Taj.

Everyone was welcome, both to watch the games and to take part in them. It never occurred to him to restrict cricket games to only the male, talented players; Singh tells me that 'I'm an old-time cricketer, but I'm progressive in my thoughts.' Living away from their parents for the first time, some of the girls in the university dorms were emboldened to try cricket, with tennis-ball games arranged for them on the football pitches and in the sports halls. At home in India many students had only played cricket with a tape-ball or tennis ball and played their first hard-ball games in Ukraine.

The cricketers usually remembered to be quiet when appealing, but from time to time they really got into trouble. Singh remembers: 'Students would come from all over Kharkiv with stumps and bats in their hands.

The police used to stop them; sometimes they even took them to the police station, and I had to go and get them out from there. They thought the players were going to a fight or something.'

By this time Hardeep Singh had become a well-known figure in Kharkiv, and his connections with the city's authorities helped to resolve any misunderstandings between the cricketers and local residents. Singh's contacts also offered him a smoother wicket for his players to play on – the outdoor basketball court in Kharkiv's beautiful Gorky Park. In later years the authorities gave Singh permission for the Indian students to also celebrate the Hindu festival of Holi in Gorky Park each spring. In the autumn he would organise their Diwali party in one of the city's clubs.

In 2000 he set up the Ukraine Cricket Federation. This made him the first man to have grown up in the city of Jalandhar to become the head of a national cricket board. The second was an old team-mate of his, Anurag Thakur, who was briefly president of the Board of Control for Cricket in India (BCCI) from 2016.

In 2000 Singh also made contact with Thamarai Pandian in Kyiv. The pair began to arrange tournaments in the capital together, with the Indian businesses – and the omnipresent powdered drink MacCoffee – giving them a few thousand dollars for promotion, uniforms and prizes. In the first years of the decade Singh always brought a strong team up from Kharkiv, prepared for an inevitable final against Pandian's Kyiv Cricket Club.

Cricket games between Kyiv and Kharkiv, Ukraine's modern and old capitals, mirrored one of the country's biggest football rivalries. For decades the 'ultras' of Dynamo Kyiv and Metalist Kharkiv exchanged hostilities whenever the teams played each other. The mood in the stadiums changed suddenly in 2014 when Putin sent troops from Russia into eastern Ukraine. After that, matches between Dynamo and Metalist played out to the noise of both groups of fans bellowing the same slow, venomous chant: 'Putin *khuylo*.'

The rivalries on the cricket pitches were still mostly between Indian-born players, but Singh and his vice-president Thamarai Pandian took steps to address this. Singh remembers: 'In about 2003 we thought about properly involving Ukrainian cricketers. From 2006 we had a rule that each team had to have one Ukrainian. It was around that time that we got to know Wayne [Zschech] and Yura [Yuri Zahurskiy]. Wayne used to bring players from his church to Kyiv, and we would divide them into our teams.'

Making domestic cricket more inclusive and representative was an important step towards Ukraine being accepted into the ICC. If her neighbours

Hungary and Romania could become members – not to mention places like Gibraltar and Cyprus – why couldn't Ukraine? With a population of over 40 million people and a deep sporting culture, by any measure Ukraine was an ideal candidate to become Europe's next Associate nation.

'Only in 2013 and 2014 did we start thinking seriously about it,' Singh says of Ukraine's journey towards ICC membership. 'The problem we were facing was that these things needed a lot of money. But meanwhile my business was going up, so I had extra money to spend. First I re-laid the pitch at the ground in Kaharlyk, because for the ICC norms you can't have a concrete pitch; the bounce has to be variable.' With a new high-quality astroturf wicket, Kaharlyk CC became the home of Ukrainian cricket, where the national team could play its international matches.

With an acceptable ground to play on, the next thing the federation had to do was set up a proper domestic league. 'We made a Ukraine Premier League [UPL] in 2018,' Singh tells me. 'We used to first invite players for trials before selecting them. And then we did a mini-auction to divide the players. We invited players from all over Ukraine. We used to fund their travel, accommodation, food and kit. There were a minimum of two Ukrainian players in a team. We had the rule that if you were playing as a batsman, you had to come at two-down; or if you're a bowler you had to bowl a minimum of two overs.'

The six teams in the UPL were all sponsored by Ukrainian companies; Faisal Kassim's BobTrade Super Kings played against the Global Focus Royal Thunder, the NixTour Falcons, the Ananta Riders, the Makeway Tuskers (captained by Abdul Vahab), as well as Mohammad Zahoor's Istil. In the first edition there was also a team representing the pharmaceutical company Eurofast. The auctions made sure that the squads were roughly as strong as each other: captains would select their all-rounder first, before taking it in turns to pick the rest of their players.

While the seasoned cricketers relaxed before the matches began, the Ukrainian players were given another 30 minutes to practice. Even though the extra nets didn't translate into many runs or wickets, they impressed the seniors with their attitude and work ethic. And the Slinko brothers, Seryozha and Vova, were worth their places in the teams for their fielding alone.

Singh shows me a promotional video that the UCF had recently made, blending together games in Kharkiv, Kyiv and Kaharlyk. It was filmed and professionally produced by Binil 'Zack' Zachariah, set to a soundtrack with an adrenaline-soaked drumbeat.

The aerial shots from Zack's drone show players in coloured uniforms; in one scene they are all running on to Kaharlyk's parched outfield, with a long white marquee on the boundary.

All the scenes capture the evocative aesthetic of Ukraine in the summertime: deep blue skies, dark green trees, and rows of concrete housing blocks. Against these backdrops, a group of schoolchildren does some batting and fielding drills on a football pitch, and a victorious senior team, in lime green and grey jerseys with 'BobTrade' on the front, does a lap of honour with a gold trophy.

On an astroturf wicket on one unkempt field, an Indian seam bowler with a slingy action lets go of the ball with genuine speed, which his compatriot scythes through the air towards the boundary with a ferocious cut shot.

The video shows several of the older Ukrainian cricketers in action; with so many computers and phones left behind and now lost in the war zones, this is rare footage. In it, Veniamin Zahurskiy, Yuri's youngest son, about 20 years old, is taking throwdowns from his father on the sidelines of one of the grounds. A left-handed batter, like Yuri and their coach Wayne Zschech, 'Venya' pops the ball easily off the middle of his Indian-branded bat.

In another clip, this time on the astroturf pitch in the middle of the ground, Yuri bowls a flat off-break from around the wicket, and Veniamin takes a step forward and taps a drive into the covers. It is the bowling action of fifty-something dads the world over – and a nurdle into the off side that hesitant club batters the world over score most of their singles with.

There are soundbites in three languages. Yuri, his hand on Veniamin's shoulder, says in Ukrainian: 'I've been playing cricket for ten years. I think my time is coming to an end, but there is a new generation, which I think will be even better.'

Hardeep Singh himself states in English: 'We want to have a [national] team of native Ukrainians in the near future, maybe even by next year'. In Russian, Dr Alok Bansal, a longtime champion of cricket in Kyiv, says: 'There is a chance, hope, a dream, that Ukraine will play in a World Cup one day'. Originally from the Indian state of Uttar Pradesh, Dr Bansal is one of Ukraine's top surgeons, and the founder of the Indian-Ukrainian Friendship Society.

Towards the end, pastor Wayne Zschech, in a bright green helmet and holding the same bat that Veniamin had been using for his throw-downs, says in English: 'Let's develop cricket in Ukraine!'

An Indian player in an orange Eurofast jersey also speaks to the camera. He talks in sentences that use Ukrainian and Russian words at random: it is not a mistake, or something hard to understand, but a Ukrainian dialect called *surzhyk*. He speaks it flawlessly.

Taking its name from a Ukrainian bread made with two kinds of flour, *surzhyk* is mainly spoken in the east of the country, in the Kharkiv, Luhansk and Donetsk regions that are closest to Russia. The cricketer would have picked up the dialect in the years before the Kremlin's brutality in Ukraine, when Russian language and culture was an accepted part of life almost everywhere.

The video finishes with still photos of an awards ceremony, where Thamarai Pandian and Hardeep Singh present a jersey to Shyam Bhatia, the patron of the Ukraine Cricket Federation who had flown in to watch the tournament. The montage fades out with the words: 'Vision of UCF: Self-belief and conviction to make dreams come true'.

Another of Zack's films that has survived is a highlights video from the first Ukrainian Premier League in 2018. Set to an upbeat dance song, and with lingering aerial shots of Kaharlyk's parched yellow field and perfect blue sky, it captures the essence of long summer days in Ukraine.

At the start of the video Wayne Zschech is playing cricket with a group of Kaharlyk's boys and girls on the field's astroturf wicket. A boy of about 11 in a black t-shirt runs up and bowls a slow, flighted leg-break at an older boy. The ball pitches a bit short, just outside the stumps, and spins and bounces a lot. It would have been a testing ball – but of course, being a pupil of Zschech and Yuri Zahurskiy, the older boy is batting left-handed, and pulls it hard through square leg.

The next ball the boy faces is from another older boy, wearing the blue cotton t-shirt with the yellow *tryzub* symbol on the front. He skips to the crease and rips an off-break with a smooth action. It comes out short and flat; Zschech, already wearing his yellow NixTour Falcons jersey, collects it behind the stumps. Then the video cuts to Thamarai Pandian putting medals over the children's heads.

The atmosphere is just as warm when the footage of the main tournament begins. Players from all six teams mix together in the marquee on the boundary as they watch the games. Indian and Ukrainian children play together by the boundary ropes.

But on the field the players are going hammer and tongs to win the cup for their team. Bowlers charge to the wicket and hurl yorkers at the wooden springback stumps; batters hit powerful drives, or launch sixes into

Wayne Zschech's cabbage patch at long-on. Every run is run hard.

In fading light a batter in the orange and blue of the Ananta Riders plays the winning shot in the final, a cut through point. He leaps in the air, before his batting partner runs to embrace him. It is getting dark by the time the presentation ceremony and group photos happen, with relaxed hugs and happy faces all around. No wonder Faisal Kassim had called that week blissful.

Throughout the video Yuri Zahurskiy appears in a NixTour Falcons jersey, offering handshakes and bear hugs. But it was another Ukrainian, Oleksiy Lyubchych, who won the inaugural UPL in 2018 with the Ananta Riders. He made some headlines too; after the final Lyubchych told the *Kyiv Post*: 'My heart kept stopping for the last 50 minutes of the match, and then sped up so fast that my chest almost exploded.'

Truth be told, it wasn't always the feel of leather on willow that enticed the Ukrainians to take part. Hardeep Singh used to pay the Ukrainian cricketers a match fee of $20 to play in some of his tournaments. At a time when the average salary in Ukraine was about $100 a week, cricket was one of the more fun ways that young people in Kaharlyk could earn some extra money. It was thanks to incentives like these that a few years earlier Yuri Zahurskiy had become Ukraine's first professional cricketer.

But still, there were plenty besides the Zahurskiys who played cricket for love, not money. Some of them led such entertaining lives that a weekend passion for T20 cricket was hardly the most eccentric thing about them. By day Oleksiy Lyubchych is a manager at a life insurance firm, but in his spare time, as well as being the Ananta Riders' all-rounder, he is a stand-up comedian, a screenwriter and an actor. In September 2022 a short film that he wrote and acted in, called *Liberal*, about Russian attitudes towards Ukrainians, premiered at an art museum in Odesa.

In July 2018 a group of players that called themselves the Ukraine national team travelled to a competition in Poland, known as the Euro T20 Cup. The tournament featured teams representing Poland, Hungary and Switzerland, as well as Ukraine. It was not sanctioned by the ICC, so the eligibility requirements were very lax; Yuri Zahurskiy travelled with the squad to Warsaw but was not selected for any of the games. Nevertheless, the team still featured five players with Ukrainian passports.

The side, selected from the top performers in the UPL, made it to the tournament's final. In the last match, at a sports club in the town of Stare Babice on the outskirts of Warsaw, they came up against Hungary's de facto national side.

Fielding first, Ukraine's change bowler Saket Malik, a pharmaceutical marketer and a NixTour Falcon, took 3-13 from his four overs, as Hungary were bowled out for 128. In their chase the senior batters in yellow and blue enjoyed mixed fortunes: Wayne Zschech scored 28 off 31 balls from No. 4, while Hardeep Singh, batting at six, was lbw for three. But the innings that won the cup came from a Ukrainian citizen at eight.

Majid Gul was born in Pakistan, but had been settled in Kyiv for many years, also working for a pharma company. He played his cricket for Thamarai Pandian's Kyiv Cricket Club and for a couple of teams in the UPL. Hardeep Singh had selected him for the touring team for his medium-pace bowling, which brought him mountains of wickets on Kaharlyk's bouncy pitch. But that day he starred with the bat.

On strike with two overs remaining and 26 runs needed to win, Gul hit a four and a couple of twos from the first three balls, to leave Ukraine with 18 to score from the last nine. With only the tailenders to come he pummelled the next three balls for six, to win the match, and the Euro T20 Cup, with a full over to spare.

As proud as Gul, Saket and others felt to wear the yellow and blue jersey, for the ICC to recognise the national team many of the Asia-born players needed to be phased out, and replaced by cricketers who had learned the sport in Ukraine. Until the Covid-19 pandemic hit the country in 2020, Singh and Kobus Olivier were working on plans to create a pathway from the cricket being played in Kyiv's private schools to the clubs of the UPL.

To make sure that local cricketers kept developing, one of their ideas was to invite more cricket coaches from India to hold nets and coaching clinics in all of Ukraine's cities. The UCF had received enough equipment from Shyam Bhatia's Cricket for Care initiative to think about hosting cricket fairs not only in Kyiv and Kharkiv, but also in places like Odesa and Lviv.

The cricket lessons would be accompanied by Hardeep Singh's massively popular Indian picnics. Takeaways from his India Palace restaurant had become a huge part of cricket culture, not only for the players, but for the Ukrainian supporters who came to watch. Many of them were the players' families, and staff from local consulates.

'Food was also provided free of cost,' he explains. 'We tried to make the most of every day at cricket. We used to play a minimum of three T20 matches a day, and sometimes even four. So we used to bring all the teams to the ground very early. The teams that came early for the first match got breakfast at the ground, and the teams that came in the afternoon, we used to give them food also.

'It was just so they wouldn't worry about anything, like in England, when you play on a Sunday and everything is organised.'

So keen were Hardeep Singh and Thamarai Pandian to get Ukrainian cricket up to speed with the international game, that in 2019 they did something that not even the Indian Test team had yet done: their teams faced each other in a day/night match, played with a pink ball under floodlights in a park on the eastern edge of Kyiv.

In 2021, the year before the invasion, Hardeep Singh took out a lease on a seven-acre plot of land outside Kharkiv. Over several months he turned the field into another ground for Ukraine's national team to use in the future. 'It was a dream project,' he says, showing me a photo on his phone of a picturesque oval. The field sits in a shallow basin, so spectators could sit on grass banks all around the ground. The land sits on top of a raised mound, so that there is a view of the city beyond one of the boundaries.

'I gave all of my summer to that ground,' he adds. 'In one year I put $50,000 into it. We played a lot of cricket there.' Fittingly for such a labour of love, the field was located just off Volonterska (Volunteer) Street.

It was a sign of the progress that cricket had made in Ukraine that Singh was able to lay a cricket square on what used to be a rugby union pitch. Rugby is a much more developed sport in the country: the Ukrainian Rugby Federation has been a member of the International Rugby Board (IRB) since 1992, and runs established leagues for men's, women's and youth rugby teams, as well as a big Sevens set-up.

At the time of the invasion in February 2022, Ukraine's men's rugby union team was 37th in the IRB world rankings – within touching distance of Germany, who play against Georgia and Portugal in the Rugby Europe Championship. The women's Sevens team took on France and Scotland on the European Sevens circuit in 2019, and have been ranked as high as 22nd in the world.

Hardeep Singh had similar ambitions for Ukrainian cricket. Once Ukraine's ICC membership was finalised, his idea for the country's first official internationals was a five-team T20 tournament at his new ground in Kharkiv, where his guests would be their old friends from Poland, Hungary and Switzerland, plus a budding team from Latvia.

Singh's model for developing domestic cricket in Ukraine in the last decade had been the IPL. But listening to him talk about organising his first international tournament – putting the teams up in the best hotels; plying the visiting players with the best food – I wonder if he also sees himself as a modern-day Kerry Packer, the influential Australian businessman who brought colour and glamour to the World Series Cricket that changed the white-ball game in the 1970s.

In the end, the Russian invasion forced Hardeep Singh to put all his cricketing plans on hold. This has at least been welcome news for his wife and daughter, two Ukrainians who he never managed to convert to cricket. Until this summer, he tells me with a smile, they would always go on their holidays without him, while he stayed behind in Ukraine to play in tournaments.

They call for him in the lobby, to start a day's sightseeing in London, and they step out on to Westminster Bridge together. We had talked all morning, but he barely mentioned the awful days four months earlier. Only months later did Binil Zachariah tell me that Singh did not leave Ukraine until he knew that all of his students and staff had themselves got out safely.

Chapter Six

†

THROUGHOUT UKRAINE, in churches and graveyards, and by the side of the road at the entrances to towns and villages, stand Eastern Orthodox crosses. Usually they bear the words *Spasi i Sokhrani* ('Save and Protect') – a short prayer that Orthodox Christians say to God at moments of difficulty. Although the Ukrainian cross has not one but three horizontal lines – the lowest one is crooked, slanting down from left to right – these religious crosses look very like the symbol that denotes the wicketkeeper on cricket scorecards. This makes it fitting that the church in Kaharlyk produced Ukraine's best gloveman, 29-year-old Oleksandr Romanenko.

Sasha, as his friends know him, grew up as part of the community of the Calvary Chapel church, and was one of the first Ukrainians that pastor Wayne Zschech invited to become a 'gladiator' in his outdoor net. Wayne put us in touch in the winter of 2022, but warned me that his friend may not be willing to talk about cricket. He had been living in the war for nine months, and like everyone in Ukraine, his mind had been totally engulfed by the horrors happening in the country.

I write Sasha an apologetic message; before it was delivered I realise how insensitive it is to ask a stranger – or anyone – questions about sport while their life is being threatened. Two hours later a message comes back: 'I will be happy to chat with you …'

I write in Ukrainian, before we switch to Russian to swap messages about his early days playing cricket. 'When I was younger I used to go to the Golgotha church,' Romanenko writes, using the name that its congregation knows it by. 'One day I saw Wayne playing some kind of game in front of the church with some boys I didn't know. I was curious and went closer to watch them.

'As I was standing there watching, Wayne came up to me and invited me to join them. I had no idea what this game was, but I jumped at the chance to join in. The game looked interesting, and Wayne invited me to come to their training sessions. That's where I started to learn about cricket.'

In his long messages, full of enthusiasm even 15 years later, Romanenko's first tries at playing cricket as a 14-year-old in Kaharlyk were the same as for children in Kolkata and Canberra, Cape Town and Kent. 'At the beginning there was a lot I didn't understand. When I tried to hit the ball I usually missed it. I couldn't bowl fast, so they taught me to do it slowly, but to twist the ball as I threw it...'

By trial and error he found his place in Wayne Zschech's teams behind the stumps. He explains: 'I was usually a batter and a 'keeper. Being the *kiper* was scary the first few times – especially when the players threw the ball fast. But this taught me to keep my fear under control and have confidence that I would catch the ball.'

Fearlessness is a Romanenko family trait. Sasha's brother Vladyslav, five years younger than him, was the square-leg fielder who so badly bruised his ribs catching Hardeep Singh all those years ago. While Sasha batted and kept wicket, Vlad was more of a bowler.

Confidence also ran in the family, but on the cricket field this bravado could sometimes be misplaced. 'In one match I was batting without a helmet,' Sasha remembers, 'and one of my shots took a ricochet and the ball hit me in the teeth. I always wore a helmet after that ...'

The Romanenko brothers were still teenagers when Kaharlyk Cricket Club settled into its home ground on the school playing fields. When the teams of mostly foreign-born players began to travel down from Kyiv for weekends of cricket in the town, Sasha was making a few runs at the top of the order, and stopping the ball as much as he could behind the stumps.

Two weeks after we first speak, I ask him what his best memories are, and what role cricket had played in his life. Late that night another message comes through. 'I played in my first tournament [in Kyiv] in about 2011. I didn't play very well: when I batted I couldn't wait for the ball to come to me. I was too impatient: I just swung my bat every time and was soon bowled out.

'But with time cricket taught me patience: to think carefully, and to wait for the right moment. It's basically a game of discipline. Like Wayne used to say, it takes a gentleman's temperament.'

Zschech's Australian style of batting rubbed off on him, but the way that Romanenko approached his cricket made an impression on his opponents of all nationalities. The captain of Kyiv Cricket Club, Thamarai Pandian, would later mention to me that, besides Yuri Zahurskiy, it was Sasha among the native Ukrainians who had shown real promise as a cricketer.

Keen club cricketers all over the world would also see themselves in Sasha's behaviour off the field. 'Every time there was a tournament, each match was special to me,' he wrote one night. 'I couldn't wait for the game to start – if it was on a weekday I wouldn't go to my classes at university.' He would miss lectures at the agrarian university in the bigger town of Bila Tserkva, 60km (37 miles) from Kaharlyk, to get ready for cricket.

'Even one time when there was a match on my girlfriend's birthday I chose to play in the match, and only went to see her after the game. She wasn't very pleased that I gave so much time to cricket…'

Just as it was in Kharkiv and Kyiv, the players of Kaharlyk Cricket Club had a tradition to eat together after matches. Whether they had been playing at home or in the capital, win or lose, the team would stop at the town's branch of McDonald's on their way home.

This led to a story that follows Romanenko to this day. 'We had one player on our team, a cool guy, strong and clever and very fit, called Yuri Zahurskiy. At the start of one game he told me that if I took a catch he would buy me a Big Tasty burger.

'I don't remember which of our players was bowling, but the batter hit the ball really high and far, and it came right towards me. I wasn't a very good fielder back then, and was scared of catching the ball when it was hit hard. And the ball went so high that I could barely see it in the sun …

'I caught it. I couldn't understand how I had done it. I threw the ball away towards the hill and screamed: Biiig Tastyyyy!'

So what did cricket mean to him? 'Cricket was something new and strange,' he says. 'When I played I always felt that my team-mates were supporting me and believed in me. The game taught me to believe in myself, to fight my fears, be confident, use my head, and make the right decisions.' Wayne Zschech had wanted to use cricket to promote Christian values in Kaharlyk, teaching the importance of patience and kindness, and Romanenko came to embody these values. Just as some Christian values were helping to make them better cricketers, cricketing values – hard work and playing as a team – were making them better Christians. Or perhaps the values were one and the same.

Either way, in a part of rural Ukraine where people were trying to cope with overwhelming social and economic problems, Kaharlyk Cricket Club was never just about runs and wickets. Sasha remembers: 'I made a lot of new friends, too. I was always interested in the people from other countries who we played against. There were Pakistanis, Indians, Englishmen … In our team the players used to change all the time, and we had a lot of foreigners too. Our team was always my family.

'There were a couple of matches where I played really well,' Sasha says. 'When our victory depended on my shots, I felt that my team-mates were cheering me on. They would shout my name, and the feeling of this big responsibility gave me goosebumps all over my body. Then when the game was over, I walked off the pitch and everyone congratulated me. Even if we had lost, they knew I had tried, and given it everything I had. It's for those moments that I wanted to play, to learn, and become a better player.

'Cricket was exactly what I needed in my life. I loved the game, and I loved the people I played with. And I really value and respect Wayne; I'm so grateful that he appeared in my life.

'I want to tell you as much as possible,' his message ends. 'But it's hard right now to remember more.'

Sasha had already told me more than enough. It's hard for him to remember more because he is now a sniper in the Ukrainian army.

Romanenko was writing to me from a military base in Estonia, where the Armed Forces sent him to train over the winter of 2022. Since the first day of the invasion he has been serving in the military, protecting Kaharlyk and other towns from Russia's assaults.

Romanenko isn't a wicketkeeper anymore. The cross by his name now stands for the Orthodox crucifix on the roads outside Ukrainian villages; it is these lands that he is now risking his life to save and protect. The wicketkeeper symbol, in any case, is not actually a religious cross: it is a dagger, borrowed from genealogical texts, where it symbolises death.

Like the majority of Ukrainians, Romanenko felt a deep anxiety in the first weeks of 2022, as the threat of the Russian invasion became more and more real. Like almost everyone else, he hoped until the very last hour that it would not happen. But at 4am on 24 February, like tens of millions of his countrymen, he was awoken by dozens of messages on his phone, telling him that the war really had begun.

That morning the authorities in towns and cities all over Ukraine began summoning men to join the territorial defence. But Sasha Romanenko, his brother Vlad and their friends didn't wait for the call: they went to the Bila Tserkva office of the territorial defence to volunteer themselves. When they got there at dawn there was already a long queue of men waiting to do the same.

The next morning, as their first command in the territorial defence, the Romanenko brothers began to build checkpoints at the entrances to Bila Tserkva, and roadblocks in the centre of the town. They were given weapons, and briefly shown how to use them.

At the start of the invasion it became known that Putin had planned to take Ukraine in a matter of days. He appeared to believe what he was told by his inner circle about the government in Kyiv being infiltrated by Russian-hating Nazis, and assumed that the people of Ukraine would welcome Russian troops with open arms. The brainwashed young soldiers expected to be treated as liberators when they crossed the border.

The reality was very different. On the same days that Kobus Olivier had watched from his apartment window as frail old ladies threw Molotov cocktails at Russian soldiers, Romanenko also witnessed the people of Bila Tserkva giving everything they could to fight the invaders back.

'Everyone came together', Romanenko writes from Estonia. 'People brought us food – even ordinary people who were passing by gave us something to keep us warm and something to eat. I stood at the checkpoint for about three weeks. But this wasn't enough for me. My hate took over me – for the people who were attacking Ukraine, destroying homes and entire towns, killing and raping people.'

In his late twenties and in perfect health, Romanenko felt he could do more as the invasion turned into a full-scale war than standing at a checkpoint.

'I wanted to help the country and our people by being on the battlefield. I found a volunteer battalion, called Bratstvo (Brotherhood). It was based in Kyiv. When I went there all of my friends and family were worried about me. They asked me not to do it. But I had already made my decision.'

The game taught me to believe in myself, fight my fears, be confident, use my head, and make the right decisions...

Romanenko could have ended up in the army earlier. While at school, around the time he started going to nets in Kaharlyk, he spent some of his weekends at youth camps that had a military aspect to them. As a teenager he dreamed of joining the Spetsnaz – the army's special forces, a military unit that Ukraine (and most other once-Soviet countries) kept after gaining independence in 1991.

The younger Romanenko would have made a good soldier – 'it's my character to protect people; I have always stood for honesty, fairness and loyalty' – but the Ukrainian army in the early 2000s was in a weak state. Its budgets were pilfered by corruption in the governments of Viktor Yuschenko and Viktor Yanukovych, meaning that training was very poor. Romanenko instead chose to continue his studies, enrolling on a five-year degree course at Bila Tserkva National Agrarian University. After he graduated, seeing that there were few jobs to apply for, he travelled a few times to Germany to earn his money there.

In his mid-twenties, when he finally took the step of trying to join the army, he was rejected as too old. By 2022, at the time of the invasion, Romanenko had started a business with a friend, equipping the Ukrainian fire service with technology that extracts smoke from buildings. The business had begun to bring them big profits.

Bratstvo, the volunteer battalion in Kyiv, housed its new recruits in student dorms at the city's prestigious Taras Shevchenko National University. Romanenko shared the living quarters with hundreds of other Ukrainians – as well as some foreigners who had come to fight for Ukraine. The more experienced fighters were sent straight to the battles around Kyiv, to defend the towns of Bucha, Irpin and Hostomel that were being obliterated by shelling. But Romanenko couldn't join them: his intake of volunteers was left behind to be trained by military veterans from the United States, Great Britain and Poland.

In joining Ukraine's territorial defence forces, he was taking the same steps as athletes like Serhiy Stakhovsky, the former professional tennis player who was once ranked 31 in the world. As Ukrainian men of fighting age went to defend their country in the first weeks of the war, the Romanenko brothers joined several thousand other sportspeople who either signed up for the territorial defence forces or were already serving in the Ukrainian army at the time of the invasion.

In April 2023 Reuters reported that 262 Ukrainian athletes were killed in just the first year of the war, either as civilians, or while serving in the Armed Forces. Most of these athletes were amateurs: before the horrors of February 2022 they also had full-time jobs or studies, while competing as some of the best in Ukraine – and often in Europe – in their sports.

Yevhen Malyshev was part of Ukraine's biathlon team at the 2020 Youth Winter Olympic Games in Switzerland. He died defending Kharkiv in the first week of the invasion, just before his 20th birthday.

Oleksandr Suprunov was a champion kick-boxer, winning several international championships. He fought during the siege of the Azovstal steel plant in Mariupol, one of the fiercest battles in the first months of the war, and died soon after.

Hryhoriy Barchyshyn played football for the reserve team of the Ukrainian Premier League team Karpaty Lviv. At the start of the war he joined the territorial defence, and later became part of the Ukrainian army. He evacuated wounded comrades and performed combat operations in eastern Ukraine. During one of them, near the village of Popasna in Luhansk region, his car was hit by an enemy artillery shell, which ended his life in May 2023 at the age of 38.

Artem Azarov won boxing competitions in the Kharkiv region and in national championships. He was also a talented landscape artist. Having already served in the army for five years, he died in March 2022, at the age of 26, from a mortar attack while defending Kharkiv.

Liudmila Chernetska was a bodybuilder from Odesa. She was pregnant when she and her husband were killed in a rocket attack that hit their apartment block.

Kostiantyn Deneka was a road cyclist for the Citroen team, who was aiming to represent Ukraine at the 2024 Olympic Games in Paris. He served in one of the Ukrainian army's special forces units and was killed in the town of Bakhmut in March 2023 at the age of 28.

Oleksandr Sukhenko was a 25-year-old footballer, who played as a striker for the amateur team FK Kudrivka outside the city of Chernihiv. While serving in the territorial defence Oleksandr distributed aid parcels to the residents of Kudrivka. He died after helping to evacuate several people from the town.

Serhii Pronevych was a long-distance runner, who in 2019 ran a marathon in four hours and 36 minutes wearing full military gear. In the first weeks of the invasion he acted as a lone volunteer, running dozens of kilometres each night around his town of Boromlia, in the Sumy region, to scout the position of the Russian invaders, and report back to the Ukrainian territorial defence. It is thought that he would also set fire to any Russian tanks or armoured vehicles that he came across, using Molotov cocktails that he made during the day, and took with him in a backpack on his runs. Eventually Russian soldiers used thermal imaging cameras. When they found him they tortured and killed him.

While thousands of Ukraine's amateur and semi-professional athletes were defending their country, the governing bodies in Europe's major sports were making sure that her elite sportspeople could still represent Ukraine in global events.

In the very first days of the war the 48 members of Rugby Europe, the association that organises most of the continent's rugby union tournaments, launched a fundraising campaign to keep Ukraine's national team and domestic championships going throughout 2022.

FIFA, football's global federation, changed its rules to allow foreign players living in Ukraine to temporarily join clubs in other countries. The European body, UEFA, allowed Ukraine's national team to play its home games in Poland for the foreseeable future. UEFA's charity 'Foundation for Children' also donated

€100,000 to provide humanitarian aid to children injured in Ukraine, and refugee families who had fled to neighbouring Moldova.

The Lawn Tennis Association (LTA), which governs British tennis, banned Russian and Belarusian players from playing at its events in 2022, so that Elina Svitolina and other Ukrainian players would not have to play against them at Wimbledon. The LTA and the All England Lawn Tennis Club jointly gave £250,000 to the British Red Cross and the 'Tennis Plays for Peace' initiative, to support Ukraine's refugee response efforts.

In late March and April, when the fighting around Kyiv died down, some of the recruits from the Bratstvo battalion travelled east to Kharkiv, where there were still battles. Others left the battalion.

Sasha Romanenko wasn't sent anywhere in those months. Feeling that he was no longer needed, he left the Bratstvo battalion. But he didn't go home: he walked out of the university dorms and went straight to the Ukrainian army's main recruitment office. He spent the day of 8 May, his 28th birthday, there with a friend, waiting to be given their *viyskovi kvitky* – the military identity cards that would allow them to enter official Ukrainian military bases.

The military recruitment office sent him to the base of a brigade. They arrived there on 9 May – the day of the year when, in a horrible irony, Russians and Ukrainians traditionally mark Victory Day against Nazism, and honour their grandfathers' sacrifices fighting together in the ranks of the Soviet army.

'There were already a lot of people at the base, and there was nowhere to sleep,' Sasha says. 'One night they put us in a basement; it was very cold, damp, and it stank.' But it wasn't so far away from the life in the Spetsnaz that he had thought about as a child: 'They assigned me the role of sniper,' he says. 'One little dream had come true. Our battalion was put through training for a while; then they sent us to Chernobyl, where the invasion from Belarus was coming from.'

On occasions he writes about his military training in the same enthusiastic way that he had described his first times batting in the net in Kaharlyk. After Chernobyl, he tells me, 'they sent us snipers to train at sniper school. It was really cool.'

Romanenko spent the following months in intensive training at a series of camps. 'Several times we were supposed to go to the battlefields,' he writes, 'but something always changed. I began to feel as if fate herself didn't want me to end up on the front lines.' At the beginning of 2023, as the final step before the Armed Forces sent him to the war zone, Romanenko was sent to Estonia to be trained further as a sniper.

The next time Sasha writes to me he is in Kharkiv. As the war ground into its second year, he had made it to the front lines, as he wanted. At the end of the winter his battalion was moving through the east of the country, coordinating assaults on Russian forces in towns that the 'orcs' had occupied. He mentions being ordered to shadow a tank brigade and undertaking training exercises with them. He also mentions a time when his unit refused to follow their commander's orders to attack a group of oncoming Russian tanks, because they did not have the weapons to stand up against machine guns.

He tells me that whenever he has rest periods, he opens one of the books that he brought with him to the front lines. In Kharkiv he was reading Thomas Keneally's *Schindler's List*. At the same time as Russian state propaganda was spreading the idea that Ukraine's army was stocked with Nazis, here was a soldier, who at home in Kaharlyk referred to the Sri Lankans and Indians he played cricket with as his family, reading a book that sheds light on the evil of Hitler's Nazi Party.

Kharkiv is a drastically different city to the one it had been before the invasion. Until it was hit by thousands of missiles, the place that Hardeep Singh, Faisal Kassim and others had called home was a busy city of over a million people, which had been a centre for Ukrainian art and literature, as well as sport.

In Bakhmut, Romanenko's unit was regaining control of a water-pumping station when they were surrounded by Russian soldiers. He and his colleagues were saved from death by the Ukrainian special forces, who forced the Russians to retreat and brought their own people to safety. 'Everything isn't going as well as they're telling you on TV,' he writes.

Another time, in the countryside outside Donetsk, his unit went to collect some weapons that they thought the Russians had left behind. But when they arrived at the location, they were ambushed by 50 gunmen. On this occasion Romanenko's unit were accompanied from the start by the Ukrainian special forces in armoured vehicles, but this time, the special forces had to retreat when they realised the ambush. The team were left on their own, armed only with guns that were 40 years old.

Romanenko and his colleagues waited for the Russians soldiers to come closer, then killed them all. 'How many I have killed with my own rifle I will say later,' he says. 'It's a story for another time.'

But with time cricket taught me patience: to think carefully, and to wait for the right moment. It's basically a game of discipline.

Until 2014, when the Kremlin began to control eastern Ukraine, Bakhmut was called Artemivsk. It was an unassuming provincial town, and almost always known by its Russian name, Artyomovsk. Ukrainians knew it for its sparkling wine factory, which produced the bottles of sweet Artyomovskoye 'Champagne' that no birthday or New Year's Eve party in Ukraine was complete without. The town of Bakhmut doesn't exist any more. In his messages, Romanenko calls it "hell".

It was in Bakhmut, the old Artyomovsk, that Sasha Romanenko and other Ukrainian soldiers came up against the most notorious Russian fighters. In the second phase of the war it became known that when soldiers contracted to the Russian military were killed in the most dangerous zones, they were being replaced by convicts released from Russia's high-security prisons.

These conscripts had joined the private mercenary group known as Wagner, which Putin denied was a formal part of the Russian army. Any Wagner fighter who survived six months in Bakhmut, or other battlefields, was freed to go back to the Russian towns where they had committed their violent crimes.

While he was in Estonia I had asked Romanenko for some more of his cricketing memories. Weeks later he remembers, and sends me a message one night from Bakhmut. 'As strange as it sounds, what I want to be doing most of all right now is playing cricket. Sweating and getting tired at a training session; the ball hitting my legs or body. But I have a sniper's rifle in my hands right now instead of a bat, and a grenade instead of a ball.'

Chapter Seven

PLAYING AND MISSING

WHATEVER PLANS 32-year-old Anna Murochkina had for 2022 as she celebrated the New Year at home with her family, they didn't include teaching children to play cover drives in a park a thousand miles from home. But in a twist of fate, in taking her small daughter Varvara out of Vinnytsia, 250km (155 miles) south-west of Kyiv, to Croatia to escape the attack on her city, she became Ukraine's first qualified cricket coach.

We speak in the summer of 2023, over a year into the war. Anna is back in Ukraine, working as an analyst and stock manager at the retail company where she had worked before the invasion. She video-calls me one evening as she is driving through Vinnytsia, and shows me the centre of the city, just after dark. There is not a soul on the streets.

Having to uproot Varvara, not yet two years old, from their home was an awful shock. 'It was very difficult to process what was happening to us,' she says. 'War was something from books, or from the stories our grandparents told us. My choice to leave my homeland came to me after two months of Russia's attack on Ukraine. The decisive factor [in leaving] was, I started hoping that a rocket would instantly kill me and my daughter, without us suffering. Realising that these are not normal thoughts, I left for Croatia.'

Although she speaks good English, Anna chose Croatia because its language has words that Ukrainian speakers can understand. A story goes that Croatians can trace their roots to the Carpathian Mountains in what is now western Ukraine. Leaving Vinnytsia on a train, Anna comforted herself by telling Varvara that they were going to meet some of their very distant relatives.

When they arrived in Zagreb several days later, and tried to get used to their new surroundings, the reality of what was happening hit her. 'It was very hard with a baby,' Anna says. 'I was looking for [other] mums like me, so that I would not be lonely, and have some psychological support. [One day] while walking in Zrinjevac Park I heard some familiar words; when I turned towards the shouting I saw some kids playing.

'I didn't know what game they were all playing, and I became interested. I approached a group of mothers and asked them what was happening. That's when I first heard about cricket. I decided that I should definitely come to the next training session and try to play with my daughter.'

Having left behind a life of fitness training, yoga and swimming in Vinnytsia, Anna wanted to do more than just watch the children play. 'I started to help organise the games on the field,' she explains. 'Oliver [Kobus Olivier] only spoke English, so the children did not always understand what they needed to do. I began to translate, and at the same time study the rules of the game. I'm a mother of a little girl, so I got along with everyone.'

By the time the Murochkinas arrived in Zagreb, the boxes of cricket kit donated by the Lord's Taverners charity in London had already been delivered to the cricketers of Zrinjevac Park. The extra plastic bats and stumps – serendipitously all in Ukrainian yellow and blue – meant that Olivier, with Anna his equally enthusiastic sidekick, could supervise several games at the same time.

Anna contacted some people at cricket clubs in England, and arranged for them to send some clothing that would fit the children. It was a very unexpected twist that their old shirts and caps, with the badges of clubs in Buckinghamshire and Staffordshire, would have a second life kitting out new cricketers from Ukraine, who a month earlier hadn't known what the sport of cricket was.

Anna wasn't satisfied with just letting the children have a hit. When it came to learning cricket, she took a very studious approach to mastering the game, just as Yuri Zahurskiy had once done in Kaharlyk. 'In order to teach the children properly, I decided to take the ICC's Foundation course, and get an international certificate that would allow me to teach soft-ball cricket anywhere in the world.'

If the idea of a young Ukrainian refugee, the mother of an infant daughter, studying for an ICC coaching course sounds unlikely, then Anna had more than just sporting reasons for doing it. She could feel how much the children were struggling, away from their homes and separated from their fathers, and she could see how the exercise and new friendships were helping them to cope. The evenings spent playing cricket together had the potential to be a vital support network for the children – but as Kobus Olivier continued to spend the last of his money on pizzas for them, they couldn't rely on him for much longer.

'Having international recognition,' Anna says of the coaching certificate, '[I hoped] it would be easier for me to ask for help to support the Ukrainian children, not only as their representative, but also as a certified coach.' With two people from the Ukrainian cricket family now spending time with the children during the week, the pair wrote to the ICC's Europe office at Lord's, to ask for a small grant to keep the cricket sessions in Zrinjevac Park going. They did not get a reply.

With agonising news still coming daily from their home towns, the setback was the least of anyone's worries. The children kept coming to the park with their mothers; Olivier and Murochkina kept teaching them the basics of cricket, and with every session the boys and girls with the plastic bats and Sussex caps began hitting the ball further and bowling it straighter.

Anna mentions: 'While their fathers were fighting for peace in Ukraine, protecting our homes from Russian attacks, the children in Croatia were playing hard cricket, showing how hardy and invincible they are. Their example was their fathers; they are very proud of them.' Her own little girl was too young to understand what was happening, but Varvara was taken to Croatia without a chance to say goodbye to her father, who had to stay in Ukraine.

Anna used the cricket games to teach the children lessons about life. She tells me the story of one young boy in the park who was overweight. When it was his turn to bat one day, the boy who was bowling at him started to make fun of his size. When the ball came to him, the batter tried to retaliate by hitting it straight back at the bowler – but instead the ball flew upwards and hit a bird that was flying past.

Everyone playing the game stopped in horror as the bird fell to the ground, but after a few seconds it got up and flew off. Murochkina gathered all the children together to explain that it is wrong to bully people who are different – but it is also wrong to respond to taunts with aggression.

Not everything they did in the park was 'hard cricket'. Anna sends me a video of her doing 'keepie-uppies' with a bat and a tennis ball, laughing with a girl of about 12. Many of the children were too small to know what game they were playing. In another video the 18-month-old Varvara is chasing a boy of the same age around the park with a blue plastic stump. In one photo Anna shows me, the little girl is looking unimpressed as her mother, padded up in bright yellow pads and gloves, tries to hand her a mini Kookaburra bat. Other videos show a huge picnic, with children and adults sitting around pizza boxes.

As a way for the children, their mothers and grandparents to socialise, get some exercise and eat hot food, cricket in Zrinjevac Park made a huge difference to their lives. And in Anna Murochkina they had the perfect coordinator, hugely empathetic to all children, and at the same time perhaps the world's most unlikely cricket obsessive.

'It is very hard to organise games with small children who have been in a war,' she says later. 'They have all become victims of the Russians' invasion of Ukraine.

'They all had to leave their old, comfortable lives behind, in order to save their lives. You can't talk to them in too loud a voice; you can't give criticism, or tell them they are doing something wrong. They are already heroes and winners.

'That's why our games of cricket weren't only about bowling the ball and hitting it the right way, but also psychological support for every child. In Zagreb we thought up a course to teach cricket from A to Z. Every session was planned and prepared in detail: a warm-up, some practice in groups, a game, and at the end, after all their efforts, pizza for all the children.'

Word of the games in Zrinjevac Park spread beyond Zagreb's new Ukrainian community. One evening local television reporters came to a session to film a segment about the refugee cricketers for Croatia's biggest news channel HRT. Their games were shown on the evening news that week. On another day the British ambassador to Croatia, Simon Thomas OBE, came to the park to meet the players.

All of the Ukrainians in Zagreb were missing their families and homes, and many of the people who came to the cricket sessions were suffering with serious trauma. Anna remembers one of the most painful cases. 'One day a new player came to us – a girl who had been through something awful. A Russian missile hit the building she lived in. Unfortunately the building was destroyed, and with it her childhood was destroyed too.

'When she arrived to us she was extremely timid; she just stood to one side, hugging herself and watching us play. There was a light in her eyes that gave away that she wanted to play cricket too – but when some of us came to her and invited her to join the game, she refused. She just wasn't ready to. I decided to come over to her and tell her a little about cricket, to put her mind at ease.'

The story echoes how Wayne Zschech had spotted Sasha Romanenko watching him play cricket in Kaharlyk many years earlier and invited him to join in – but as a conversation between two refugees in a park in Croatia, the way that Anna encouraged the girl to come out of her shell was incredible.

Murochkina remembers: 'I started talking to her about the history of cricket: how it was born in the south of England in the 16th century, and by the end of the 18th century had become one of the most popular sports there. I told her that the expansion of the British Empire allowed it to spread across the world, and that the first Test matches between countries were played in the middle of the 19th century. And even though cricket isn't very well known outside the countries of the old British Empire, in countries with a total population of over two billion people, it's like a religion.'

Anna's idea was to take away any negative thoughts the girl was having. She went on to tell her about some famous films that show cricket being played: *The Beach* with Leonardo di Caprio; *Syriana* with George Clooney and Matt Damon; *A Good Year* with Russell Crowe and Marion Cotillard; *The Best Exotic Marigold Hotel* with Judi Dench and Dev Patel; there is even cricket in *The Chronicles of Narnia*. Anna had read that the iconic actress Sophia Loren once joined in a game of cricket while staying in England to film one of her movies. She even explained to the girl why England and Australia play for a trophy that is a little urn filled with ash.

It worked. The girl eventually came on to the cricket pitch with Anna and had some turns bowling the ball and hitting it with a bat. In the end she became such a good player that she began to help Anna to teach the other children.

In the first months of 2022, as over 10 million people flooded in a panic through Ukraine's western borders, tens of thousands of volunteers from Europe and beyond came to the crossing points to bring them clothes and other supplies and to help them find places to stay. The volunteers came from all walks of life; among them was one former international cricketer.

Stuart Meaker played a handful of white-ball games for England at the start of the 2010s. In a long career he took almost 300 first-class wickets for Surrey, and was one of the fastest and most intimidating bowlers in English county cricket. After retiring from the professional game at the end of the 2021 season he bought a campervan and spent the following winter fitting it out, with the idea of spending some time travelling around Europe in it.

He changed his plans in February 2022, when he saw television footage from Ukraine of pregnant women and small children being evacuated from the towns outside Kyiv where massacres were taking place. He decided at that moment to drive his van to one of the border points, and began loading it with medical supplies, nappies and other provisions.

A Polish community group in south London told Meaker to deliver his supplies to an address in the town of Lublin, an hour from the Ukrainian border. The only sleep he allowed himself during the thousand-mile drive was on the ferry after leaving Dover, and in a McDonald's car park somewhere in Germany.

When he arrived in Lublin, he dropped off the supplies at the address he was given in London, and went straight to a shopping centre to fill up the campervan again. The next morning he drove on further, to the border crossing in the town of Medyka. He didn't have any plan for what he would do when he got there, but having seen the Ukrainian orphans arriving in Lublin with his own eyes, he was ready to do whatever he could to help.

At the border he found that he was needed by a team that was rescuing dogs and cats. After doing that for a while Meaker drove the van to another border town, Przemyśl, where he helped out at a refugee centre.

Writing in *Wisden Cricketers' Almanack* after he returned home, Meaker said: 'I came face to face with the consequences of a war zone – the most intense experience of my life. People talk about returning soldiers having a thousand-yard stare. I saw that in the eyes of civilians. People were arriving on foot, with one bag; the children clutched teddy bears. One person was dropped off on a stretcher – we didn't know who they were, or what treatment they needed. I've never seen anything like it. One of the priorities was to treat people for stress. A lot were given panic medication, just so they could function. It was only a couple of weeks of my life, but it still hits me hard. I know now what people mean when they refer to the realities of war.'

Six months later Meaker was back playing cricket again, for an England Legends side in a series of T20 exhibition games in India. In a twist of fate, in his first match, against Sri Lanka Legends, he bowled at Jeevan Mendis, whose experience of Ukraine only a few years previously had been so overwhelmingly different to his.

As Meaker was helping at the refugee centre in Poland, a small fraction of displaced families escaping Ukraine had the resources to make it as far as Croatia. Through the Ukrainian grapevine in Zagreb I make contact with Khrystyna Zaitseva, another of the mothers who had been part of the cricketing evenings in Zrinjevac Park. Khrystyna begins writing in good English, but she soon asks to switch to Russian. Until the war this had been the first language of most people in the eastern half of Ukraine, albeit spoken with a distinctive, soft Ukrainian accent.

Khrystyna and her six-year-old son Roman have moved to Zagreb from the town of Kramatorsk, in the Donetsk region. Like millions of other people in Ukraine, on 24 February 2022 Khrystyna and Roman were woken by explosions at 4am. Realising that the

Thamarai Pandian presents the trophies after a tournament at Kyiv's Voskhod stadium, as Yevheniia Tymoshenko and Sean Carr look on.

Cricket in Kyiv's Syretskiy Park during mayor Vitali Klitschko's summer sports festival.

Schoolchildren with cricket sets from Shyam Bhatia's Cricket for Care initiative. Mr Bhatia is pictured in the blue and yellow shirt.

Pastor Wayne Zschech (left) and Yuri Zahurskiy, batting partners at Kaharlyk CC.

Middle practice on the field at Kaharlyk CC.

A BobTrade Super Kings team photo at Kaharlyk CC, featuring Yuri Zahurskiy (back row, second from right) and Faisal Kassim (front row, furthest to the right).

Oleksandr Romanenko batting.

An early Kaharlyk CC team photo.

A match at Hardeep Singh's cricket oval in Kharkiv.

Faisal Kassim.

Hardeep Singh (right) presenting a trophy in Kharkiv.

Hardeep Singh's cricket oval in Kharkiv.

Anna Murochkina and her daughter Varvara in Zagreb's Zrinjevac Park.

Pizza in Zrinjevac Park after a cricket session.

Catching practice in Zrinjevac Park.

Anna Murochkina batting in Zrinjevac Park.

Wayne Zschech during a humanitarian mission in the town of Borodyanka, June 2022.

Yuri Zahurskiy taking people out of the town of Bucha, 2022.

Binil, Yulia and Emily Zachariah on a platform at Kharkiv's Naukova metro station, February 2022.

The children's safe room at Naukova station. February 2022.

Oleksandr Romanenko, October 2023.

The basement of Faisal Kassim's dormitory building, February 2022.

invasion had begun, the mother quickly grabbed their passports and a few belongings, before they ran out of their apartment.

She took them to the train station, but by the time they got there she hadn't worked out where they would go. Numbed by the eight years of fighting that the towns around Donetsk had already been subjected to, and with some savings that they could use, Khrystyna and Roman kept travelling west, until they eventually stopped in the little town of Nova Gradiška, in the south of Croatia.

Their idea was to wait in Croatia for a few weeks until the violence in eastern Ukraine stopped, then go back home. But after five months of the war Khrystyna's savings had almost run out. She moved with her son to Zagreb, so that she could find a job, and Roman could find a school.

In the capital she heard about the cricket games in Zrinjevac Park from another displaced Ukrainian. It was still summer, and Khrystyna, a fitness instructor, wanted her son to get some exercise.

'It wasn't just cricket practice,' Khrystyna writes of the evenings in the park. 'It was like a team-building exercise. Because what brings people together more than a common problem? There were lots of us at the sessions. We could always make new friends with people who had the same interests, share new information about life in Croatia, and do something useful with our time. We learned to live again.'

From the very first session both she and Roman enjoyed the new game: 'In cricket it's important to have good reactions, throw the ball with accuracy – and you also need to run fast. It's a lot of activity, together with some thinking: the perfect combination.'

The efforts of Kobus Olivier and Anna Murochkina didn't go unnoticed. 'The coaches really got the children involved,' Zaitseva writes. 'Looking at my child and the other children, I could see how much they were concentrating on the games. Not all of them were old enough to understand what they had to do – but they were so tenacious in the way they ran and hit the ball.

'The game was something new for us; none of us had heard about cricket before. We only started playing to take our minds off what was happening in Ukraine. Emotionally it was a very painful time for us.

'But playing cricket really did interest us. I play sport myself and love being active. The children also understood really quickly what the game was about. The teams take it in turns to hit the ball into the field, trying to score as many points as possible, or to stop their opponent from scoring points. It really is absorbing.

Players need to use not only their physical skills, but also to think quickly as well.

'The children were so happy playing with the bat and running, counting up the points. Nothing brings people together faster than a shared goal and idea.'

With their home town of Kramatorsk almost completely destroyed, mother and son have stayed in Zagreb, where Roman is settling into his first year of school. I ask Khrystyna whether Roman could tell me his best memories of playing cricket in the park. She gets back in touch a few days later: 'He says the thing he liked the most was when we all ate pizza together after the training sessions. And also running after the ball. But then, he is only seven ...'

'Cricket will stay in my heart,' she says at the end of our conversation. 'The game came into my life at the best possible moment. I'm grateful to the organisers for thinking about us Ukrainians. In our situation, support and encouragement can come from just some kind words.'

A couple of months later I manage to get in touch with another of the families from Zrinjevac Park. The mother is also called Anna; she and her ten-year-old son Artem are now living in Canada but stayed in Zagreb for a few months after leaving Kharkiv.

Their escape from Ukraine was harrowing. 'My family left Kharkiv early in the morning on 24 February, when they began to open fire on our city,' Anna tells me. 'We left our car in a garage, and a friend took me, my son, husband and our cat out of the city. It was frightening. We heard a series of explosions coming from somewhere. Everyone was in shock: only the day before everything had been quiet and peaceful, and people were just going about their lives.

'My parents didn't come with us, because they believed it would all be over soon. After the first gunshots there was a lot of traffic, and queues at petrol stations, because a lot of people didn't think that the war would really happen ...'

'It was hard to get out of Kharkiv. After a while we managed to get out and headed for the west of Ukraine. It's a long way, plus sometimes they closed some of the roads. We had to spend a night in a village outside Vinnytsia. That night there were planes flying overhead; it was frightening.

'At the end of the next day we reached Lviv. We could stay there in a special hostel that my son's school had been given access to. We stayed there for a couple of days, then rented a place ourselves. But every day it became more frightening. My husband sent me, our son and cat to Poland.

'In Poland we stayed in a refugee camp. It was okay there, but still it was no place for me with a child.

We left for Krakow, where my husband's sister lived. From there we decided to go to Croatia; in Poland they were already running out of accommodation for Ukrainians. I had been to Croatia when I was young, and I remembered that the people there are very kind.'

Anna continues: 'In Croatia we didn't know anyone. Artem didn't want to be on his own, and I was really upset. And then in one of my group chats I saw an invitation to the cricket sessions for Ukrainians, and we went along. It was there that we made some new Ukrainian friends. After that we went to cricket three times a week. We could all talk in the open air and do the training. Cricket gave me a chance to distract myself a little bit and come out of my depression.

'The adults introduced themselves to each other and talked. Each of us told the story of how we ended up in Croatia. We also swapped information with each other about all sorts of things. These evenings brought us together. It meant a lot to meet other people from my city and remember the home we had left behind.'

I ask Anna what her favourite memories are of playing cricket. 'The best thing for me was that my son found some friends there. He could take his mind off the news, off the war, and the situation that we found ourselves in. [In the park] he was smiling and felt happy.'

Before we say goodbye, Artem sends me a short voice-note. 'It was good because my friends were there,' he says. 'And they taught me to play cricket. I like playing it.'

Chapter Eight

MISSED CHANCES

AS KOBUS Olivier lay in his bathtub in February 2022, listening to the bombings outside Kyiv, he was taking calls from the ICC's Europe office. The messages coming from Lord's at the start of the invasion, and as the war continued into March and April, were reassuring. Ukraine would still be confirmed as an ICC member at the council's next meeting in July. No one knew how long the war would last. If the Russian army could somehow be repelled, then Ukraine's cricket family – and millions of other displaced Ukrainian families – could all go home that summer.

But still, as the summer's Mediterranean Cricket League approached, the players and coaches who were invited to compete in it were scattered across the world. Olivier was on a humanitarian visa in Croatia; Faisal Kassim, Thamarai Pandian and many others were recuperating in India; Wayne Zschech was in Australia, gathering donations for villages on the front lines; Hardeep Singh was working from Dubai; and Binil Zachariah and his family were staying in Canada. Every one of them planned to come back to Ukraine – even if it wouldn't be to the homes they had left behind.

Of the many reasons they all wanted to return to Ukraine, cricket was one of the most important. The MCL in July, at Zagreb's Budenec Oval, would be the first time that they played together as a recognised national team. If the team could hold their own against some strong European club sides, they could use the experience to prepare for their first ICC tournaments.

Within a few years, at the rate they were going, Ukraine could enter the European qualifying groups for the men's T20 World Cup, where they would meet teams like Italy and Denmark. With all T20s between the ICC's Associate nations counting as official internationals, this would give them several matches to train for each year.

Resting at his parents' home in Kerala, Faisal Kassim was determined to wear the yellow and blue jersey when he got back to Ukraine. On another call from Tbilisi, he tells me that two days after arriving in

India following his ordeal in Kharkiv, he was thinking about cricket again.

Kassim left the hostel in Poland to fly to Delhi on 9 March. On 12 March he heard about a district-level T20 competition beginning near his home town of Thodupuzha. He had missed the registration deadline for the player auction, but when the organisers learned about his situation – and the five years he had spent at the Kerala academy in Kochi – they quickly found him a team to play for. Running off his aches and pains from the nights sleeping on the basement floor, Kassim took four wickets as his team reached the semi-finals.

Although he had lived thousands of kilometres away from India's south coast for the past four years, playing cricket in Kerala again he felt as if he had never left. While he was in Odesa and Kharkiv he kept in touch with many of his old team-mates and coaches, and they had all supported him as he recovered from his spinal injury to start bowling again.

The people of Kerala have always supported their cricketers going to different countries to play. Many of the young men who don't make it as professionals keep playing the game while working or studying abroad. This is usually in the United Arab Emirates – Kassim's childhood friend KM Asif was working at a bottling plant in Dubai, living in a room with seven others, when he came home for IPL trials – but sometimes they find themselves further afield as well. Faisal knows cricketers from the academy who ended up playing cricket in Malta.

The group of boys who Kassim played his cricket with before leaving for Ukraine, Asif included, became some of the best players in India. Sachin Baby and Basil Thampi are mainstays in Kerala's Ranji Trophy team, and have played first-class cricket for India A. Sanju Samson, Rajasthan Royals' captain, has taken a step further, to become a regular in India's white-ball squads.

Many of the schoolboys who were chosen for the Vijay Merchant Trophy in the same year as Kassim are now also elite players. Batter Devdutt Padikkal has played T20 games for India, and pace bowler Kartik Tyagi toured Australia with the Test squad in 2020. Wicketkeeper Dhruv Jurel and batter Nikin Jose have been called up to play for India A.

But it is Samson whose career Kassim has followed closest of all; their paths often crossed in junior cricket, and they knew each other well. 'We were in the same complex at the Kerala Cricket Association,' Faisal explains, 'so I met him many times at practice sessions and matches. And I used to go and see him play in his home town. I bowled at him when he came to play at a ground in my district. From that time onwards he was very busy with the Ranji Trophy and other things; he didn't play much local cricket...'

As the BobTrade students came home to their various parts of India, cricket tournaments in several states began to feature players who Hardeep Singh was lining up for the Ukrainian team. The cricketers played wherever they could, to keep in shape before the trip to Croatia in July. In the spring of 2022, while Tyagi and Samson were playing in the IPL, Faisal and the other students from Kharkiv were going to the grassroots maidans in their old stomping grounds.

'We all had regular practice,' Kassim explains. 'In India we had more opportunities to play. There were so many games: practice matches, under-25 district matches, selection matches, and so many club tournaments. Every Saturday and Sunday we were playing in tournaments, either hard-ball or soft-ball.'

Bonded by what they went through together in Ukraine, the students who had shared dorms in Kharkiv kept in contact, even when their return to India took them hundreds of kilometres apart. 'We were all in touch with each other,' Kassim says. 'We had some WhatsApp groups, a Facebook group, and we were all planning to play more tournaments together. We thought that even though the war was going on, we could play in some European tournaments [in the summer]. We were all practising very hard at that time, because we were on the verge of joining the ICC.'

Despite the distance between them, in April four of the cricketers who would play for Ukraine's national team – Kassim, his cousin Abdul Vahab, and their friends Muhammed Junaid and Govardhan – met up in Kochi to play in a cage cricket tournament. Meanwhile in the neighbouring state of Tamil Nadu, a group of players who knew each other from Kharkiv National Medical University entered a team in a cricket league for doctors and other medics.

In May a message from Hardeep Singh caused a stir in the squad's Facebook group. That year's edition of the Ukraine Premier League would be held not at Wayne Zschech's ground in Kaharlyk, but in Delhi. Singh had booked a venue to play day/night matches under floodlights, and threw open the invitation to any cricketer who had ever studied in Ukraine.

Hardeep Singh meant well, but with the Mediterranean Cricket League on the horizon, what Ukraine's best cricketers needed was to be playing together as a team, not competing against each other. At about the same time, Shyam Bhatia, the veteran steel tycoon and the patron of the Ukraine Cricket Federation, stepped in.

Bhatia kept in touch after our meeting in Mayfair. One day he tells me about an idea he had to support the squad. 'I offered to bring Ukraine's cricketers to Dubai that summer,' he says. 'My idea was to send coaches for their players to train in Dubai, and for them to have matches all over the UAE.'

Throughout his 45 years in the Emirates, Bhatia has wielded a lot of influence over cricket in Sharjah and Dubai. He had often sponsored unknown players that caught his eye in small tournaments, and placed them in high-profile leagues. He wanted to do the same for the Ukrainian team: the players would use Dubai as their training base and play practice matches there, before being flown to Croatia for the MCL.

In the end, neither Singh's tournament nor Bhatia's invitation was able to come to life. By June the war in Ukraine was only growing more violent. The students who had left Kharkiv would not be able to go back to their universities; they had to quickly find other courses, either in India, or, as Faisal Kassim chose to do, through the new BobTrade programme in Georgia. There was no chance of anyone being able to travel to Delhi for a week, let alone to Dubai.

Kassim, Abdul Vahab, Muhammed Junaid, Govardhan and the other players finally went their separate ways. Their dream of playing for Ukraine in the MCL, testing themselves against Simon Katich and Brad Hogg, came to nothing.

A month later Ukrainian cricket was gone for good. The blow that destroyed its 30-year history did not come from a mortar shell to a pavilion, or a landmine on an outfield, but in an email. At the ICC's annual meeting in July, four months after the start of the war, the governing body announced its newest intake of Associate members. Ukraine was not one of them.

The council's press release explained its decision in cold sporting terms: 'In light of the ongoing war there is currently no cricket activity taking place in Ukraine. Consequently [...] the Ukraine Cricket Federation does not currently meet this aspect of the Membership Criteria.'

The annual grant of $18,000 from the ICC would have kept the cricket sessions running for the hundred or so Ukrainian children who came to Zagreb's Zrinjevac Park, and perhaps allowed the federation to buy out the lease on the old rugby ground in Kharkiv, which Hardeep Singh had put so much work into bringing up to ICC standards. With Singh battling to save his businesses as the Russian invasion destroyed his city, he couldn't have kept the cricket ground alive with his own funds.

No sport can survive in a country at war without support from its governing body. If Ukrainian cricket could have been protected for a few years, until peace returned, then it could then have grown on its own, with support from the government and corporate sponsors. Ukraine's rugby union team, as a member of the International Rugby Board, has partnerships with several national companies, and support from the ministry of sport. There was no such help available to Ukraine's cricketers.

Kobus Olivier was philosophical when talking about the trauma of his escape from Kyiv. But when he starts to talk about the ICC's rejection there is bitterness in his voice. 'They said that because of the war they were going to continue supporting us,' he tells me. 'But there's been no contact, no support; zero [assistance] from them with any of the refugee programmes. We were thrown under the bus – up to today that's what I believe.'

'To an extent I understand why they couldn't follow through with giving us membership. We were in a state of war, and because of that we didn't have a home ground. The whole league fell apart, all the Indians left, so there would be no domestic cricket whatsoever. So, I can understand that we didn't meet the criteria in the middle of a war.'

'But then I also look at it like this: every sport has criteria to belong to the world governing body, like FIFA [for football]. All other Ukrainian sports teams – tennis, football, swimming – that are affiliated to the world governing body, not one of them *lost* their affiliations or memberships because of the war. Everybody understands it's a war.

'To an extent, I understand why they didn't give us membership. But they could have given us *something*.' Olivier gives a political example. At the start of the invasion Ukraine was not accepted as a member of the European Union, but was elevated to 'candidate' status, which will allow the country to interact more closely with the EU until it is ready to join.

Ukrainian cricket's videographer Binil Zachariah shares Olivier's feeling of betrayal. Zack is another gently spoken man who was deeply hurt by the ICC's decision. He had told me from Canada: 'The work, the effort, the time we spent on developing cricket in Ukraine is not something that can be ignored because of a freaking war.'

Olivier feels that cricket's status as a tiny sport in Ukraine counted against it. With sports that are popular in the country, governing bodies have been more flexible with their rules. He says: 'The Ukrainian junior football set-up, all their junior teams from under-10 to under-18, they moved here to Croatia, funnily enough. They've got a hostel and school in Split. They just moved their whole set-up from Kyiv, and for the time being all their junior football is based in Croatia.'

The world of cricket has rallied round its Test-playing teams when their countries have been struggling. 'It's a bit like Pakistan,' says Olivier of Ukrainian cricket's forced exile. 'When there were problems in Pakistan and they couldn't play games there, they were based in Dubai.' Afghanistan, too, were given Full Member status in 2017, but because of the situation there they have not played any matches in the country.

There are holes in all of Olivier's arguments. While cricket in Ukraine dissolved at the start of the invasion with the exodus of its Asia-born community, professional football has battled on. The Ukrainian Premier League is still being played, with air raid sirens often forcing players into the changing rooms in the middle of matches.

Teams from cities close to the front lines have stayed in the country; Zorya Luhansk now play their home games in Kyiv, and Shakhtar Donetsk are based in Lviv. And while Pakistan's national team couldn't play Tests at home for a few years, domestic tournaments were still able to continue there.

The impact of the rejection on Ukraine's cricketers is only half of the story. In turning its back on the players in Kyiv, Kaharlyk and Kharkiv, didn't the sport of cricket lose something too? For $18,000 per year, from the ICC's expected annual earnings of $600 million, a sport with Sasha Romanenko and Faisal Kassim in it – not to mention Anna Murochkina, Roman Zaitsev, Daryna Pyatova and others – would surely have been worth the investment.

'Our men's team was bloody good,' Olivier says. 'I watched those guys play. Let them play in India – send an MCC team to play against them. Send a Middlesex Invitation XI to go and play against them. Encourage them, keep them going,' As well as memorable matches, the players would have given the organisation some welcome PR. He adds: 'What an opportunity that would have been for the ICC, to be seen helping Ukrainian cricket. Can you imagine the fuss they would have made over a Ukrainian junior team playing a few soft-ball matches in the UK?'

Providing that this war can be stopped eventually, the governing body has missed the chance for Ukraine to be the sport's next inspiring story. Afghanistan's rise in the last 15 years has shown that miracles do happen in the world of Associate cricket. When the Afghan team made its first appearance at a global tournament, at the 2015 50-over World Cup in Australia and New Zealand, only six years earlier they were battling in the lower reaches of the ICC's structure, travelling to games against the likes of the Cayman Islands and Argentina.

For Ukraine to have put herself on the same trajectory, Olivier believes that the first step would have been for the Ukrainian mothers living abroad to take coaching courses, just as Anna Murochkina had done when she arrived in Zagreb.

If a country where all the cricket coaches are women sounds far-fetched, there is no doubting the success that cricketing mums have had in South Africa. Olivier had seen this in action while travelling with his mentor Bob Woolmer, as he helped the much-loved coach to introduce cricket to new parts of the country. 'In South Africa,' he explains, 'the female teachers in the black townships are the soul, the glue, of the mini-cricket programmes.'

In Olivier's vision for Ukraine, the displaced mothers and their children could have brought cricket back to Ukraine from the United Kingdom and elsewhere in Europe. 'After the war we could have had an influx of, say, 300 soft-ball qualified coaches, going to cities all over Ukraine. And then 10,000 kids that were exposed to cricket in other countries. If they go back, you've got coaches, you've got children; you've got cricket. It's a unique opportunity, and the ICC missed it completely.'

In England at least, communities are introducing Ukrainian children to the game, giving them a fun way to settle into life in their adopted country. 'Last time I checked there were more than 150,000 Ukrainian refugees in the UK,' says Olivier in the summer of 2023. 'Lancashire is starting a mini-cricket programme for the refugee kids, incorporating them into the Lancashire cricket set-up. And all the counties have cricket structures; you could just copy-paste that programme to all the other counties. There could be 20,000 young Ukrainian kids playing cricket in the UK, getting top coaching at top facilities.

'After this war, when it finishes one day, of all the kids that have played cricket, half of them will go home to Ukraine. This is a unique opportunity, but they were not interested.'

Olivier's vision of a post-war, cricket-mad Ukraine is optimistic in the extreme – but it does have a precedent, in another nation whose diaspora learned to play cricket while escaping from war. The Afghanistan team that joined the ICC in 2014 were drawn from players who had grown up with cricket in refugee camps in Pakistan during the Afghan-Soviet War in the 1980s. Their successes allowed cricket to grow in Afghanistan itself.

If the idea of Ukraine's cricketers following in Afghanistan's footsteps is too fantastic, they could have emulated a more modest success story. It comes from Croatia itself. The Croatian cricket team has been an ICC Associate since 2017, and its men's side plays T20 internationals against the likes of Italy and Greece.

The team has very few South Asian expats, and always has a core of ethnic Croats: the captain and wicketkeeper is Grzinic; for years the best batter was Vujnovich, and Turkich bowls first-change. But behind Croatia's scorecards there is another story: these cricketers learned the game in Australasia, where some of their parents and grandparents emigrated during the Yugoslav Wars in the 1990s.

All of the cricketers selected to wear Croatia's 'Baggy Red' have played at the highest amateur levels in Australasia. John Vujnovich was born in New Zealand, and used to play for Auckland's Second XI. Daniel Turkich played first-grade cricket in Australia, as did the Grzinic brothers, Jeff and Michael, who grew up in Perth before moving to their parents' homeland.

All are proud Croatian citizens, and work hard to help cricket to grow in Croatia. Jeff Grzinic is the man behind the Mediterranean Cricket League, which he created in 2016.

Before the Yugoslav Wars, Oceania's call for immigrants in the 1960s indirectly led to several Slavic cricketers playing for Australia and New Zealand. Before Simon Katich, Michael Kasprowicz, Jason Krejza and Anton Devcich there was the fearsome Macedonian bowler Leonard Durtanovich, who was one of the fastest men to ever play the game. Because of racial prejudice in Australia in the 1970s, Durtanovich kept his real name a secret from the cricket teams he played for. He took his 64 Test wickets under the pseudonym of Len Pascoe.

With the cricket culture that Hardeep Singh, Wayne Zschech, Thamarai Pandian and Kobus Olivier had built since 1993, if Ukraine had been recognised as a cricket-playing country, and been given some support during the war, what could the next 10 years have looked like for its players?

Could Daryna Pyatova and some other talented female cricketers – who their coach was sure could become a force in world cricket – have one day found places in T20 franchise teams? One league they could have played in is the FairBreak Invitational Tournament, which is open to cricketers from the ICC Associate world.

At the tournament's second edition in 2023 two Brazilian all-rounders, Roberta Moretti Avery and

Laura Cardoso, were team-mates of the West Indies captain Deandra Dottin, and English wicketkeeper Lauren Winfield-Hill. Mariana Martinez, a pace bowler from Argentina, played alongside South African batter Mignon du Preez; and Japan's Shizuka Miyaji was the spinner in a side whose all-rounders were Sophia Dunkley from England and Pakistan's Bismah Maroof.

The annual FairBreak tournament proves that even cricketers from the smallest of the emerging cricketing countries can hold their own against the world's best. In one of the matches in Hong Kong, du Preez and the Australian batter Phoebe Litchfield were both dismissed by the skillful Bhutanese left-armer, Anju Gurung.

Until Ukraine was ready to enter the European qualifiers for T20 World Cups, bilateral series for both its men's and women's squads could have been arranged with its neighbours Romania and Turkey – or with Sweden, who in 2023 were being coached by Kobus Olivier's old gym partner Jonty Rhodes. Perhaps the 16-year-old Pyatova and a couple of promising Ukrainian boys, spotted playing cricket in Lancashire or another English county, could have been sponsored for some kit and extra coaching through Shyam Bhatia's Cricket for Care initiative, as Mumbai's Sarfaraz Khan had once been.

If the Ukraine Cricket Federation had support from the ICC, could Rhodes have been tempted to coach the men's teams, based in Dubai or Croatia? There would surely have been no shortage of big sponsors wanting to align themselves with the players' journey. Or could the seniors from Kyiv cricket's heyday, wherever they are now, have persuaded Marvan Atapattu to take Ukraine forward? Before coaching Sri Lanka Atapattu cut his teeth in the world of Associate cricket, working first as Canada's batting coach, then as coach of Singapore.

In the end, while the big dreams faded away, even the little ones could not get off the ground. Soon after the ICC's rejection, Kobus Olivier thought up a tournament for his young cricketers to play in. The Ukrainian Freedom Cup in Zagreb would see them play soft-ball matches with teams of schoolchildren from Croatia and the neighbouring countries. But when he contacted various national cricket boards to ask for some funding, no one was prepared to sponsor it.

Autumn 2022 saw the last games of cricket in Zrinjevac Park. 'We had to stop this programme,' Olivier explains. 'It is one of the saddest things I've ever done. When winter started it started getting dark at four o'clock. We didn't have a place to play indoors. I went to see three or four venues we could have used, and got quotes, but the ICC didn't see fit to support us in any way.'

The British Embassy in Zagreb offered to pay for the children to play indoors for a month, but that only would have delayed the inevitable. Like Faisal Kassim and his friends a couple of months before, the Ukrainian cricketers of Zrinjevac Park were forced to go their separate ways.

Chapter Nine

OVER

THE CHIRPING of birdsong floats through a meadow at dusk. Over the sound of the pipits come two low, echoing thuds of missiles being launched. In the video, one of the shells is visible in the left of the frame, a little flash of white rising in the evening sky. In July 2023 I check in with Sasha Romanenko; underneath the video he writes: 'The orcs are shooting their artillery at us. In two days others are coming to take us away from our positions.'

In August he writes again: 'Right now we are undertaking a counteroffensive around Belgorod. All the time we have mortars and artillery launched at us.' In the summer of 2023 the Ukrainian army began a wave of counteroffensive attacks on Russia, moving to liberate some of the Ukrainian towns that Russian troops occupied in 2022, or had controlled since 2014.

Ukraine also began to hit targets on Russian territory for the first time; Belgorod is a town 40km (25 miles) inside Russia, just over the border from Kharkiv.

He sends another video. This one shows the blackened frame of a vehicle, upside down, with dark smoke rising from it. The phone pans to a man on the side of the road in green combat fatigues; he is staring motionless ahead, his face and body frozen with shock. His beard and forehead are smeared with grease. Sasha adds: 'This is from when we came under artillery fire. As we tried to get out we drove over a mine. By a miracle we survived.' Another video, from the same location, shows that the other soldiers who were in the vehicle with them did not survive.

In February 2024 Russia's war in Ukraine will grind into its third year. There is no sign of a possible end, and little prospect of a ceasefire. The *Washington Post* has reported that Ukraine now has the most landmines of any country on Earth. It will take decades to clear them, but this process can only really begin when the war comes to an end.

'There are Russian sabotage groups trying to get to us,' Romanenko writes. 'But we destroy everyone who comes into our field of vision. As a sniper I try to always shoot with maximum accuracy, so that they all understand not to come here. I'm trying to kill 200 or 300 orcs.'

The counteroffensive by Ukrainian forces sparked in-fighting between the official Russian army and the mercenary soldiers from Wagner. In the middle of 2023 Wagner fighters stormed the Russian army's building in the city of Rostov-on-Don, and from the south of Russia marched in tanks in the direction of Moscow. The mutiny was a colossal challenge to Vladimir Putin's authority.

The coup was put down hours before the tanks reached the Kremlin. Putin met with the group's leader, Yevgeny Prigozhin. Two months after their meeting, Prigozhin died when the plane that he was flying in exploded.

I think of what Sasha had told me seven months earlier, about his feelings as he was manning the military checkpoint in Bila Tserkva at the start of the war. *'This wasn't enough for me. My hate took over me – for the people who were attacking Ukraine, destroying homes and entire towns, killing and raping people. I wanted to help the country and our people by being on the battlefield.'* As the former agronomy student and wicketkeeper spends his sixth month on the battlefield, operating as a sniper on Russian territory to save and protect his countrymen, it is time to leave him be.

As 2024 begins, cricket festivals in Ukraine are only a memory. There is hardly a trace of the game left in the places where it was once played.

Where there used to be happy cricketers sharing a barbecue at the end of a week's matches, the Calvary Chapel church in Kaharlyk is now a refugee centre. With the support of Operation Mobilisation, Wayne and Olha Zschech are able to keep dozens of displaced people safe in their spare rooms. One day, a family of five – a pregnant lady with her husband, their six-year-old daughter, and the husband's elderly mother – arrived in Kaharlyk from the city of Kherson in the south of Ukraine, which was almost totally destroyed. The family stayed with them for a year; when the baby arrived, the little boy spent his first months living at the church.

The town of Kaharlyk was spared during the first two years of the war. Russian attacks on the south of the Kyiv region targeted the nearby town of Bila Tserkva, where Sasha Romanenko used to study, and where he stood at the checkpoints at the start of the invasion. In October 2022 a kamikaze drone set fire to a building there, injuring someone inside.

There is no longer any sport played at Kyiv's Polytechnic Institute, where the capital's first cricket matches were played in the 1990s. The university is not far from the Nyvky neighbourhood where Kobus Olivier sheltered from explosions at the start of the invasion. The metro station next to the sports field was used as a bomb shelter.

The Voskhod stadium in Kyiv's Darnytsia district, where Thamarai Pandian hosted the fierce T20 leagues that Zschech and his friends eventually won some games in, is also deserted. Darnytsia, on the eastern side of the Dnipro river, suffered three significant attacks in the first 18 months of the war. In April 2022 a missile strike on the neighbourhood killed one person and seriously injured several others. Six weeks later a cruise missile hit the Darnytsia railcar repair plant. In May 2023 another missile set fire to an apartment block near the stadium.

The word 'voskhod' means sunrise in Russian. The stadium is now known instead by its Ukrainian name, Skhid.

Ukraine's English-language newspaper the *Kyiv Post*, which sponsored some of the early cricket tournaments, was sold by Mohammad Zahoor in 2018. It dissolved in 2021, but days later most of its editorial staff came together again to form a new newspaper called the *Kyiv Independent*. Since the start of the invasion the *Kyiv Independent* has been a trusted and vital information source for developments on the ground in the war zones.

The Astor school in the suburb of Mezhyhirya, where students used to watch Jonty Rhodes videos in English lessons, has been closed since the start of the invasion. The parkland around Viktor Yanukovych's old palace, including the golf course where the children used to play cricket at breaks, is now a military zone. Most of the pupils are still outside the country, and it isn't safe for the remaining children to go to school in a place that is a target for Russian attacks. The school will only be able to open again when the war comes to an end.

Hardeep Singh's new cricket oval on Volonterska Street, where he dreamed of hosting international tournaments, has not suffered any damage. But of all the places in Ukraine where cricket was played, Kharkiv has suffered the most. The city has been hit by thousands of missiles; constant shelling has turned many of the city's buildings to rubble. Faisal Kassim's university dorm on Liudviha Svobody Avenue is still standing, as is the building on Nauki Avenue where he and the junior students sheltered at the start of the war. But several of the blocks that Kharkiv's international students used to live in have been blown away.

Chapter Ten

FOLLOWING ON

IN JULY 2023 a tall and blonde Australian man appeared at a luxury yacht club in Budva, Montenegro. Middle-aged, fit and expensively dressed, the club's wealthy clientele assumed that the newcomer was one of them. But Brett Lee hadn't come to Porto Montenegro to sail a yacht down the Adriatic coast: he was looking for the cricket pitch behind the marina, where the Mediterranean Cricket League was being held for the first time.

Some of the best batters in mainland Europe were able to face Lee in that year's MCL, but sadly, none of them were wearing the yellow and blue jerseys with a *tryzub* on the chest. A recognised national team from Ukraine will surely now never take the field.

If this is the case, then Ukraine will be forever represented by 11 players who took their country to the brink of international cricket. When I try to reach them at the end of 2023, all of the players that I am able to talk with are safe. Their families are alive and well. While these bravest of cricketers will never have international caps, or player pages on ESPNcricinfo, they deserve to have a place in cricket's history.

1. Kobus Olivier

The sports teacher who came to Kyiv to get away from cricket, Kobus Olivier ended up introducing over 2,000 Ukrainian children to the game. At the start of the war his cricket lessons in Zagreb's Zrinjevac Park gave over 150 children living as refugees in Croatia a chance to play, to take their minds off distressing thoughts, and make new friends. Not long after the cricket games in the park stopped, Olivier was granted a Croatian work permit, and began a new job teaching English at a school in Zagreb.

He rues that Ukraine's cricketers were not able to reach their potential. But in the future that he imagined for them, where the women's team are beating all before them, and the men are finding their feet against their neighbours, it is hard to see a place for a coach who had supported Putin's war.

2. Wayne Zschech

The founder of the first native Ukrainian cricket team, Wayne Zschech turned a patch of land in the rural town of Kaharlyk into an international-standard cricket ground. One of Ukraine's best batters, his innings against the touring English side in 2012 was Ukraine's first recorded century.

The war has meant that many scorecards have been lost, but the country may only ever have seen two other hundreds. One was made by an unknown player against Kaharlyk CC in Kyiv a few years later, which Zschech remembered when we spoke. The last one was scored for the Makeway Tuskers in a match in Kharkiv in 2021, by an opening batter who appears in the scorebook only as 'Dany'.

The school field in Kaharlyk is no longer used for cricket, but Zschech is still bringing his community together in other ways. For years his 'Clean Soul, Clean City' initiative has provided jobs for people in a town where there are not many employment opportunities. Now he is also finding roles in the business for the displaced families who are staying at his church. This gives them a chance to support themselves and each other, while doing something that equips Ukraine with sustainable energy.

3. Daryna Pyatova

The teenage cricketer who hit the ball miles, Daryna Pyatova is one of the millions of schoolchildren whose education has been interrupted by the war. At the start of the invasion she left Ukraine with her mother and siblings. Her family have not said where she is now.

Daryna's father, the Shakhtar Donetsk goalkeeper and national team captain Andriy Pyatov, retired in 2023. He now works for the project Above All ('Ponad Usé' in Ukrainian), which organises treatment for people who suffer injuries in the war. Above All is also supported by other Ukrainian footballers in Oleksandr Zinchenko, Andriy Yarmolenko and Oleksandr Shovkovskiy, as well as the tennis player Serhiy Stakhovsky. All of the sportsmen support the project's medical centre in Ivano-Frankivsk, which provides medical and psychological assistance to Ukrainian soldiers, children and refugees.

4. Hardeep Singh

Beginning in 1993, Hardeep Singh arranged cricket matches for thousands of Indian students living in Kharkiv. When we talk by video call in August 2023, the figure reclining in bed in his apartment in Dubai is much more relaxed than the man I had met in London in the first months of the war. His family and livelihood are safe: 'Life is going fine,' he tells me. 'But that can change at any time.'

Singh could also be happier because he is playing cricket again. He often travels to India, and after 30 years has rejoined his old team in Jalandhar.

He will go back to live in Ukraine as soon as he can. He tells me that Kharkiv is also coming to terms with the invasion. After the exodus in the first months of 2022, people are coming back; there are now over a million people in the city again.

'Sometimes now [the fighting] comes into the outskirts of the city, where the infrastructure and electricity grids are,' he tells me. 'And in places like Kupyansk, near the border with Russia, something is still going on.

'Now when the [air raid] siren comes, you know what you have to do. Sometimes people know from where [an attack] is coming; from the sound they can tell whether it is coming, and how many minutes until it will strike. People have learned how to survive.'

5. Yuri Zahurskiy

Yuri Zahurskiy is still involved in bringing humanitarian aid to the towns around Kyiv. Over the last 15 years he was a mainstay in Ukrainian cricket, appearing in almost every story, and every team photo.

Kaharlyk's gentle giant was known for his batting, but an old team-mate, Abdul Vahab, remembers him for his bowling: 'Yura was a superstar bowler,' he tells me. 'Since he is unorthodox, everyone tried to hit him, but he usually got two or three wickets. And he was a great fielder: he has the biggest hands of any cricketer I have ever seen.'

Ukrainian cricket owes a great deal to Yura's hands. If he had not caught the ball so well at Wayne Zschech's barbecue all those years ago, then his friend may not have thought to invite him to play cricket with him again. And had Zahurskiy not practised for so long to become Ukraine's first serious cricketer, there might not have been a Kaharlyk Cricket Club. His sons Petya and Venya would not have taken up the game, and neither would the town's other cricketers, Sasha Romanenko, Seryozha and Vova Slinko, Oleksiy Lyubchych and many others.

6. Petro Zahurskiy

One of Ukraine's best homegrown batters, pneumonia cut Petro Zahurskiy's life tragically short in 2020 – but not before he realised his cricketing ambition. In 2012, when he had just started to play cricket, he told the BBC's *Test Match Special* that he was training to hit a six. In one of the first messages that his father sent me,

Yuri Zahurskiy said proudly that Petya 'saw the ball really well, and often hit fours and sixes.'

A player for Kaharlyk Cricket Club since its beginning, Petya also became a mainstay in the Ukraine Premier League. For a few years his innings of 56 was the highest score ever made by a Ukrainian batter. Fittingly, when Petya was overtaken on this list, it was by his younger brother Veniamin, during the second tournament played in Petya's memory. Venya may have looked hesitant in the old video of him batting against his dad, but on this day in 2021 his innings of 57 came off 36 balls.

That innings was Venya's last, and it was only the third match he ever played. From Germany he talks me through the rest of his career. 'My first game was in my home town' he says of a match in Kaharlyk. 'That day I hit my first six – the highest number of runs you can score with one hit of the ball. Even my dad didn't think I could do it.

'My second game happened spontaneously, in Kyiv. My father's team needed a player. I was really nervous for the whole game; it was an important match and I had to really concentrate.'

7. Oleksandr Romanenko

The wicketkeeper who missed university lectures and even his girlfriend's birthday to play cricket, Sasha

Romanenko was a founding member of Kaharlyk CC, and one of the best Ukrainian batters to play the game.

The last news of him came in November 2023, when he posted a photo online of a sunset over another battlefield. His brother Vlad, who also grew up playing cricket in Kaharlyk, was fighting on the front lines as well. Sasha did not mention that he had been harmed.

8. Thamarai Pandian

True to his word, Thamarai Pandian returned to the city in the summer of 2023. He now spends his time working between Kyiv and Chennai, but like Hardeep Singh he will return to his home in Ukraine permanently as soon as it becomes possible.

9. Faisal Kassim

In the summer of 2023 Faisal Kassim sends me a video of a cricket match between the Ukraine Warriors and Saffrons CC. An athletic seam bowler runs through ankle-high grass with grey housing blocks to all sides. He and all the fielders are in dark t-shirts and tracksuit bottoms.

He reaches the black matting wicket and lets go of the ball; the ball is fast but pitches short, and the batter, a left-hander in a light grey shirt, cuts it along the bumpy park. The ball goes between the legs of the fielder at point, and the video becomes shaky as the player holding the phone runs on to the field to celebrate the winning runs.

A mini-scorecard has been superimposed over the footage: in their 10-over match, the Ukraine Warriors have chased down Saffrons' 90 runs with four balls to spare. But this is not an old game filmed in Kharkiv: it is the final of the first cricket tournament ever to be held in Georgia. In another video Faisal and the rest of the players, all medical students who have relocated from Ukraine, are holding a flag with the logo of Tbilisi's Georgian National University.

As Hardeep Singh organised the first games of cricket in Ukraine in 1993, so his student Kassim brought the sport to Georgia in 2023. But the baton has not yet been passed from mentor to protégé: the videos still have all the hallmarks of Singh's vision for decadent cricket, from the smooth matting wicket and proper stumps to the matching uniforms, and medals around the winning players' necks.

Cricket in Ukraine also began on bumpy parks: could Georgia be at the start of a journey towards ICC membership? 'I don't think so,' Kassim laughs. 'We have players here, but no ground or support. And this is only with a tennis ball; we haven't played any hard-ball cricket here.'

Kassim will be in Tbilisi until he graduates in 2024. After that, he says, he will go back to India and become a doctor there. His cricketing future, whatever level he reaches again, is in India too. For now, like all of his course-mates in Tbilisi, his thoughts are still on the country he left behind. At the top of the video are the words *Slava Ukraini*: Glory to Ukraine.

10. Binil Zachariah

While he didn't play in many matches in Kharkiv, Binil Zachariah made huge contributions to Ukrainian cricket off the pitch. He gave more sleepless nights than anyone to Ukraine's application for ICC membership.

He, Yulia and Emily moved to Calgary through the Canada-Ukraine Authorisation for Emergency Travel (CUAET) programme. Like many Ukrainians who have reached Canada, Zack is now working as a customer services rep on a low salary. He hopes that his family can return to Kharkiv one day. 'If I ever get a chance for sure I will go back,' he tells me. 'Ukraine will always be our home.

'Once the war is over, we will start our plans to go back and settle in Ukraine, even if we have to start from zero.'

11. Anna Murochkina

Ukraine's first ICC-qualified cricket coach, and a teacher, in more than just the cricketing sense, to over a hundred refugee children in Zagreb, Anna Murochkina was the heart of the evenings in Zrinjevac Park.

On these evenings the children's exhausted mothers and grandparents, all of whom had evacuated their families through gunfire and bombings, could leave their children to play. Beyond the boundary, her sessions were a place for the displaced families to support each other as they tried to put their lives back together.

Anna is still in Vinnytsia, working at the retail company. Varvara, who turns four in 2024, is happy to be living at home again; she is more content on a gymnastics mat than with a cricket bat in her hands.

For Anna cricket was only a comforting memory from their time in Croatia – until the day at the end of 2023 when a children's charity called Razom My Syla got in touch with her.

The team at Razom My Syla ('Together We Are Strong') heard about the lady from Vinnytsia who helped young refugees in Croatia to feel safe by playing cricket with them. The charity wants to start a similar programme in Ukraine.

'There will be a group of 10 or 20 children,' Anna tells me one afternoon while collecting Varvara from kindergarten. 'The charity is prepared to give some second-hand equipment, and hire a sports hall, so I can teach these children to play cricket the way they do in Europe.'

Could this be the making of Ukraine's next cricket side? 'We have some really talented children', she says. 'It will be very hard on my own. But if this war ends, with some support, we could be a strong and courageous team'.

Epilogue

GUARD OF HONOUR

AS UKRAINIAN men of fighting age went to defend their country in the first weeks of the war, Sasha and Vlad Romanenko joined several thousand other sportspeople who either signed up for the territorial defence forces, or were already serving in the Armed Forces at the time of the invasion.

Since Reuters reported in April 2023 that 262 athletes have been killed in the war, many more have also died. The Ukrainians who have lost their lives since February 2022 include the following sportspeople:

Oleksandr Sukhenko was a 25-year-old footballer, who played as a striker for the amateur team FK Kudrivka outside the city of Chernihiv. While serving in the territorial defence Oleksandr distributed aid parcels to the residents of Kudrivka. He died after helping to evacuate several people from the town.

Maksym Yalovtsov played as a prop for the Aviator rugby union club in Kyiv. He was also good enough at wrestling and jiu-jitsu to win medals at European championships and was a well-known 'ultra' of Dynamo Kyiv football club. Yalovtsov was killed on the battlefield at the age of 32.

Dmytro Sydoruk won gold at the 2000 world archery youth championships in Italy. After joining the army in 2014 upon Russia's annexation of Crimea, he took the archery silver for Ukraine at the first ever Invictus Games, an Olympics-style event for wounded soldiers, in Canada in 2017. He was killed in April 2022 by a mortar mine at the age of 39.

Oleksandr Suprunov had been a champion kick-boxer, winning several international championships. He fought during the siege of the Azovstal steel plant in Mariupol – one of the fiercest battles in the first months of the war – and died soon after.

Volodymyr Androshchuk won the Ukrainian under-20 decathlon championship in 2019. In 2020 he represented Ukraine in the European under-20 athletics championship, taking sixth place in the modern pentathlon. He died on the front lines in the spring of 2022, at the age of 22.

Mykola Yaremchuk was a former Ukrainian karate champion. He died serving on the front lines as a volunteer in Ukraine's 80th airborne assault brigade.

Oleksii Tsybko was a champion discus thrower in his youth, before taking up rugby union. He won the Ukrainian league eight times with the teams Aviator and Argo-NAU, and became captain of the Ukrainian national team. From 2003–05 Oleksii was the head of the Ukrainian Rugby Federation. He was killed in Kyiv in March 2022 at the age of 55 when a rocket hit his home.

Yuri Vorona was a boxer, a regional and national champion. He died in March 2022 near Chernihiv.

Ihor Boiko played in Ukraine's American Football League, for Vovky (Wolves) from the town of Vinnytsia. He was killed on 15 June 2022 while on a combat mission near Donetsk, aged 30.

Yevhen Malyshev was part of Ukraine's biathlon team at the 2020 Youth Winter Olympic Games in Switzerland. He died defending Kharkiv in the first week of the invasion, just before his twentieth birthday.

Dmytro Sharpar was a figure skater, who competed in national competitions. Serving in the Ukrainian army in Bakhmut, he died in combat.

Oleh Sapalenko was a sambo wrestler from Kharkiv, who had won national competitions. He served as a reconnaissance sniper in the Ukrainian army and was killed at the age of 29, while on a combat mission in the Kharkiv region.

Daniel Gerliani, a wrestler from Kyiv, competed in local and national Greco-Roman wrestling competitions. He joined a defence unit days after graduating from university. He died at the age of 23, from artillery shelling in Zaporizhzhia region.

Hryhoriy Barchyshyn played football for the reserve team of the Ukrainian Premier League team Karpaty Lviv. At the start of the war he joined the territorial defence, and later became part of the Ukrainian army. He evacuated wounded comrades and performed combat operations in eastern Ukraine. During one of them, near the village of Popasna in Luhansk region, his car was hit by an enemy artillery shell, which ended his life in May 2023 at the age of 38.

Oleksandr Derevianko competed in competitions in mixed martial arts, boxing and sambo wrestling. Having joined the army in 2020, he was serving in a combat mission at the Azovstal plant in April 2022 where he came under fire and died at the age of 24.

Ruslan Piskovyi was a six-time Ukrainian champion in kick-boxing, a finalist in the European kick-boxing championship, and a silver medallist in the world championship. At the start of the war he joined the

Ukrainian army as a gunner, and died in Bakhmut from a gunshot wound aged 21.

Kostiantyn Deneka was a road cyclist for the Citroen team, who was aiming to represent Ukraine at the 2024 Olympic Games in Paris. He served in one of the Ukrainian army's special forces units and was killed in Bakhmut in March 2023 at the age of 28.

Artem Azarov won boxing competitions in the Kharkiv region and in national championships. He was also a talented landscape artist. Having already served in the army for five years, he died in March 2022, at the age of 26, from a mortar attack while defending Kharkiv.

Mykhailo Movchan was a mountaineer, who had worked in the tourism sector, specialising in mountaineering and hiking. He fought near Kyiv, Donetsk and Zaporizhzhia. He was killed in June 2023 while on a combat mission in Bakhmut.

Serhii Berezniak won several karate tournaments, including the Ukrainian national championship in 2015. He also taught karate to children at a sports club that he ran in the Kharkiv region. He was killed on a combat mission in August 2023.

Viacheslav Savytskyi played as a defender for the football team FC Kudrivka, with whom he won the Chernihiv regional cup. He joined the army at the start of the war and was killed in June 2023 in the town of Bilohorivka. He was 25.

Oleksii Druzhynets was a chess player and a children's chess coach. His children's club in his home town of Tokmak, near Zaporizhzhia, was one of the strongest in Ukraine, and won several national competitions. He was killed in March 2022 while defending Tokmak at the start of the invasion.

Oleh Bykhovets was a footballer for the amateur team Volynka. From 2022 he served as a platoon commander in the Ukrainian army. He died in April 2023 during a combat mission in the Donetsk region, aged 22.

Vitaly Merinov was a four-time world kick-boxing champion. He died at the age of 32 from injuries sustained in battle.

Ihor Osmak was a long-distance runner, who later in life became a coach to some of Ukraine's marathon runners. He died at the age of 57 in the east of Ukraine, after completing military training in Lviv that would allow him to go to the front lines.

Ihor Karuk was a decorated marathon runner, as well as a competitive rower. He died while trying to evacuate people from the besieged town of Borodyanka, outside Kyiv.

Ihor Sukhykh was a Ukrainian champion in hand-to-hand combat and won prizes in European and world championships. He also played football for the team ATO Irpin. In the first weeks of the invasion he managed to evacuate over 20 people from Irpin, but he died while doing so.

Viktor Katanchyk played floorball – a sport similar to hockey – for the Skala club in Melitopol. He was seriously injured in a rocket attack on Melitopol on 25 February 2022, the second day of the invasion, and died from his injuries soon after.

Andrii Kotovenko had been wounded near Donetsk during the war that began in 2014. He competed in the Invictus Games for injured service people and won a bronze medal in the bench press. He died in May 2022 in Donetsk.

Yevhen Obedinskyi was a former captain of Ukraine's water polo team. He was shot dead in his apartment in Mariupol in March 2022 at the age of 39.

Vladyslav Shapovalov won prizes in several weightlifting categories. He died in March 2022 when the military hospital where he was working was hit by a missile.

Volodymyr Stelmakh was a rugby player for the Rivne club. He became a lieutenant in the Ukrainian army and died in Kyiv in March 2022.

Yevhen Zvonok was a Ukrainian champion in kick-boxing, and a silver medallist at one of the

World Cups. He joined the territorial defence at the start of the invasion and died in Chernihiv at the age of 22.

Yevhen Harda was the 2011 world kick-boxing champion. He had also won several competitions in Ukraine. He died in a battle near Zaporizhzhia in April 2022.

Ivan Shchokin was a Ukrainian champion rower. He died during the defence of Mariupol in March 2022.

Alina Perehudova was only 14 when she was killed. Her house was bombed during the shelling of Mariupol. Alina had been the gold medallist at the 2021 Ukrainian weighlifting championship for under-17 girls.

Bohdan Malyuk won a silver medal at the 2018 European junior championships in Brazilian jiu-jitsu. He was also a multiple Ukrainian champion in Japanese and Brazilian jiu-jitsu, and the Kyiv champion in mixed martial arts. After joining the territorial defence at the start of the invasion, he was killed by a bomb in Kyiv in March 2022, at the age of 20.

Vladyslav Lykhoshva played amateur ice hockey for a team called Avtomobilist. At the beginning of the invasion he joined the Ukrainian army. He was killed in battle in Bakhmut in July 2023, at the age of 21.

Oleksii Dzhunkovskyi was a boxer. He won four medals at the world championships for military personnel, and later became a well-respected junior boxing coach. At the start of the war Oleksii delivered food to Ukrainian soldiers. He was killed in the gym where he worked.

Atanas Ivanov had won several weightlifting championships in the Zaporizhzhia region. He died in Mariupol at the start of the war.

Viktor Kotelevets competed in national kettlebell lifting competitions. He joined the Ukrainian army in December 2022. He was killed in February 2023, at the age of 29, while saving the lives of two of his comrades when they came under fire from a tank.

Yaroslav Mokhonko played American football for the Kyiv Patriots. He had served in the Ukrainian army since 2014. He died during a combat mission in June 2022 near the town of Bakhmut.

Yurii Luchechko had won Ukrainian competitions in powerlifting. He died at the age of 23 during the invasion of Mariupol.

Vitalii Morozov won national and international championships in kettlebell lifting. He had served in the Ukrainian army since 2010, becoming a captain. He was killed by a mine in March 2022.

Oleksandr Sheremeta coached Ukraine's junior team for sports orienteering. He was killed in March 2022 in an attack on the town of Irpin.

Dmytro Martynenko was a midfielder for Hostomel football club, near Kyiv. He died aged 25 when a bomb hit his home.

Yevhen Sliusarenko was a former champion of Ukraine in pankration wrestling. He defended Kyiv at the start of the invasion as part of a volunteer battalion. He died in a mine explosion in the Kharkiv region in April 2022.

Yehor Kihitov was a member of the Ukrainian bullet shooting team. He died in February 2022, at the age of 21, when a missile hit his building as he was defending his town.

Volodymyr Voloshchuk was a well-known powerlifter. He died while serving in the Ukrainian army at the age of 41, in a battle outside Donetsk.

Liudmila Chernetska was a bodybuilder from Odesa. She was pregnant when she and her husband were killed in a rocket attack that hit their apartment block.

Oleksandr Anikin played American football for Orly (the Eagles). He was 19 when he was killed in the Luhansk region.

Mykhailo Kravchenko was a karting coach for some of Ukraine's best drivers. He joined the Ukrainian army in 2022. He was killed in June 2023 while fighting in Donetsk region, at the age of 46.

Oleksandr Serbinov had been a medallist in the Ukrainian 400-metre and 800-metre running championships. As a member of the territorial defence he served in the east of Ukraine, where he died in a battle in the Kharkiv region.

Serhii Kolokolov was a former weightlifter who had become a weightlifting coach. He died in April 2022 while on a combat mission in Donetsk.

Mykola Poliuliak was a professional snowboard instructor, based in the town of Kamianets-Podilskyi. He went to defend Mariupol as a volunteer, where he died at the age of 38.

Ivan Bidniak had competed for Ukraine at bullet shooting for many years, winning silver medals at European championships. He was living abroad at the start of the invasion but returned to Ukraine to join the Ukrainian army. He died in a battle in the Kherson region in April 2022 at the age of 36.

Artem Mosha was a champion boxer from Kyiv. He served in the Ukrainian army and was inside the Azovstal plant during the siege in the spring of 2022. He died during the fighting there.

Oleksii Kupyriev had been a boxer in his youth, and at one time was the European junior champion in his weight category. He was killed when a shell landed in his apartment in Mariupol.

Serhii Pronevych was a long-distance runner, who in 2019 ran a marathon in four hours and 36 minutes wearing full military gear. In the first weeks of the invasion he acted as a lone volunteer, running dozens of kilometres each night around his town of Boromlia, in Sumy region, to scout the position of the Russian invaders, and report back to the Ukrainian territorial defence. It is thought that he would also set fire to any Russian tanks or armoured vehicles that he came across, using Molotov cocktails that he made during the day and took with him in a backpack on his runs. Eventually Russian soldiers used thermal imaging cameras to search for him. When they found him they tortured and killed him.

Maksym Semenov was the president of the Dnipro Cyclist Association and the Dnipro Association of Extreme Sports. He spent his life organising bike races, runs and other extreme events in and around the city of Dnipro. He died in battle.

Eleonora Maltseva was a member of Ukraine's first national women's futsal team, and won the Ukrainian championship several times with the Belychanka team. She joined the army while still a teenager, and had been volunteering to support the war effort since 2014. She was killed in July 2023 during a combat mission, at the age of 34.

Oleksandr Klepikov was a rugby union player for the Korabel club in the town of Mikolaiv, and a sergeant in the Ukrainian army. He was killed in battle in August 2022.

Oleksandr Klushyn was a mixed martial artist, who fought in 50 amateur fights and three professional ones. In 2021 he became a world champion in MMA and was awarded a blue belt in Brazilian jiu-jitsu. He had served in the Ukrainian army since 2014, and died in March 2022 in Kharkiv at the age of 29.

Viktor Yarmolenko was a former Kyiv karate champion, who was a member of the Dodzho sports club. At the start of the war he joined the Ukrainian army and helped to defend the towns of Bucha and Irpin from Russian attacks. He then served in the east of the country. He died in the town of Rubizhne near Luhansk.

Viktor Ponyatenko was a boxer in various Ukrainian national teams, and a former silver medallist in the Cup of Ukraine. He fought 120 fights in his career, winning more than 100 of them. He served in the marine corps of the Ukrainian army, and died in May 2022.

Oleksandr Popovchenko was a former professional footballer, who played for Sumy Frunzenets in Ukraine's second division in the early 2000s. He played in the country's amateur leagues until 2020. While serving as a chief sergeant in the border service he was killed in May 2022, at the age of 44.

Oleksii Yanin was a former Ukrainian and world champion in Muay Thai boxing. He had also won national championships for kick-boxing. He had been serving in the Ukrainian army since 2014 and had spent a lot of time on the front lines in Donbas. He died in Mariupol in April 2022.

Yaroslav Mamuliyev was a rugby union player for the Vitovka club in Mikolaiv. He was killed on the front lines in July 2023.

Oleh Mazur was an amateur footballer from Sumy, who played for several teams in western Ukraine. He was killed during a battle in the Sumy region, aged 26.

Oleh Prudkykh was a two-time Ukrainian boxing champion in the 60kg category, and a semi-professional boxer for the Ukrainian Atamans club. He died in battle, with little known about the circumstances of his death.

Liubomyr Bodak was a weightlifter from the Transcarpathian region, who often competed in national championships. He became a senior gunner in the Ukrainian army and died in eastern Ukraine at the age of 27.

Oleksandr Feshtryha was a six-time Ukrainian kick-boxing champion. He had served in the Ukrainian army since 2014, and was severely wounded in 2015, but continued to fight. He died in 2022 at the age of 42.

Nazar Makarenko was a Ukrainian champion kick-boxer. Having already also become a kick-boxing coach, he died in May 2022 at the age of 25 while fighting on the front lines.

Ihor Bondarchuk was a powerlifter from Vinnytsia. He went to the front lines in the first days of the war and died in May 2022 from injuries sustained in a missile attack near Zaporizhzhia.

Oleksandr Tepenchak was a sports orienteering coach from Vinnytsia. He died on the front lines in the Donetsk region during a combat mission in March 2022 at the age of 44.

Oleksiy Dyagovets was the captain of the Camelot rugby union team in the town of Chernihiv. He died in combat in July 2023.

Daniil Zvonyk was a Ukrainian karate champion, who had also won European and world titles in Kyokushin karate. While serving in the Ukrainian army he was killed during the siege of the Azovstal metal plant in April 2022, aged 25.

Vadym Sotnykov was a former European champion in hand-to-hand combat and won several other tournaments in Ukraine and abroad. He also taught children in his home city of Dnipro. He was killed on the front lines of the war, with little known about his death.

Oleksandr Pytel was a Greco-Roman wrestler from Ternopil. Having joined a machine gun unit of the Ukrainian army in 2019, he died in March 2022 in the Luhansk region.

Oleksandr Onishchuk was a former European junior archery champion. After leaving his job teaching archery at a sports school in Rivne to join the territorial defence, he was killed in May 2022.

Valery Gerasichkin played rugby union for the Credo-63 club. He was killed in battle near Bakhmut in May 2023.

Yaroslav Rudych won boxing titles in Chernihiv and the Chernihiv region. He had served in the Ukrainian army since 2014 and died in battle in 2022 at the age of 27.

Maksym Kahal won international medals as part of Ukraine's national kick-boxing team. He played rugby union for the Bastion team in the town of Kremenchuk, and also ran and practiced boxing. He died in the battle for Mariupol.

Artem Prymenko was a sambo wrestler who had won youth and senior national championships. He died in March 2022 when a rocket hit his home.

Yehor Birkun was a member of Ukraine's national mixed martial arts team. He died on 23 March 2022, on the day that he was supposed to be representing Ukraine in the MMA world championships.

Vladyslav Horbunov played rugby union for the Donetsk regional team. He died on a combat mission in Donbas aged 22.

Oleksandr Onoshko was a two-time Ukrainian rowing champion, as well as an accomplished cyclist. He was killed in Mariupol in March 2022.

Maksym Malkov competed in a multi-discipline aquatic sport called marine all-round, winning medals at international and Ukrainian competitions. He died at the age of 20.

Halyna Popovska competed in several athletics disciplines, and after retiring was a shot-put coach. She was killed in the Donetsk region in September 2022.

Oleksandr Zakolodny and Hryhoriy Hryhoriev were both members of the Kharkiv Alpinists' Club. They both died in battle.

Maksym Chumak was a judoka who had won competitions in Ukraine and abroad. He was killed at the age of 38 while serving in the Ukrainian army. A shell struck the vehicle he was travelling in.

ACKNOWLEDGEMENTS

I AM grateful beyond words to everyone who helped to bring *Getting Out* to life. Many of the people in this book kept in touch with me during an extremely difficult time in their lives.

In this regard I am grateful first of all to Oleksandr Romanenko and Yuri Zahurskiy, who found time for me while close to the front lines of the war. Wayne Zschech was also very generous with his time while he was extremely busy helping Ukrainian refugees. I am also thankful to Anna Murochkina, Khrystyna Zaitseva, Roman Zaitsev, Anna and Artem, and Veniamin Zahurskiy, for telling me their stories at very challenging times for them.

I am very grateful to the other leaders of Ukrainian cricket: to Hardeep Singh for all his help; to Thamarai Pandian for his valuable contributions; and to Kobus Olivier, for the masses of time and attention that he gave to telling his story.

Big thank yous are due to Faisal Kassim, for being so generous with his time, and so helpful in making introductions; to Binil 'Zack' Zachariah for his valuable contributions; and to Abdul Vahab Bin Habeeb for his time and advice. Without them this book also would not have been possible.

A special thank you goes to Mr Shyam Bhatia, who also made time to speak with me in person, and who has been very supportive of this book.

I am very grateful to Serhiy Rebrov for writing such a powerful and genuine foreword. My thanks also go to Dmytro Rebrov for translating the foreword, and to the Ukrainian sports journalist Andrew Todos for putting us in touch.

My sincere thanks go to everyone who helped me to put this book together. Stephen Butler, director of Strategy Council, made sure that details about the war were explained accurately and fairly. Bernard Hughes, the chairman of Chiswick CC in London, was a great help in making sure that the cricketing stories were presented as well as possible. Bruce Talbot gave some brilliant suggestions when it came to editing.

I'm also grateful to Tim Abraham (author of *Evita Burned Down Our Pavilion*), Jeff Grzinic from the Croatian Cricket Federation, Shounak Sarkar from Emerging Cricket, Tristan Lavalette from

ACKNOWLEDGEMENTS

ESPNcricinfo, Christopher Hylland (author of *Tears at La Bombonera*), Eilish Hart from Meduza, and Iryna Zeldes Le Broussois from Ukraine Charity for their advice and encouragement.